D1078586

Contents

Introduction

Listening to a family talking can be like listening to a kind of animated shorthand, filled with half-finished sentences and brief allusions: 'Remember Aunt Mary?' or 'Isn't that just like you'. So familiar to the participants is the language in which the exchanges take place, that many of them are only half listening, and they take the others so much for granted that they often do not pick up on the impact of the words being used. Maintaining an equilibrium while accommodating the family traditions, these most complex of all groups can survive by this day-to-day surface interaction, despite the fact that even the simplest statement is weighted with historical meaning. Plain facts sink beneath long-held emotions from our youth, and perceptions from childhood become unquestioned facts, which 'everyone' knows. 'You were always her favourite' and everything you say now will be measured and judged against that belief, whether true or false. What to the outsider can appear like a 'dialogue of the deaf', with no one really listening, may be a family's normal method of interaction.

Trouble can start when a family is faced with making a difficult decision that will affect them all, and gaps in awareness can become chasms of misunderstanding. What is being said can take on references far beyond the current problem, and old conflicts and rivalries may be acted out to the detriment not only of the individuals within the group, but also of the possibility of a solution being reached. Since the perspective of each family member is different, discussions can become both personal and adversarial, and 'scripts' written during childhood offer the challenge of whether we can find new conclusions to old problems. Having papered over cracks and subscribed to family myths ('Our childhood was perfect') in order to maintain some cohesion over the years, one family member may finally recognise that old battles are being fought, and worn and familiar paths are being trodden. Having perhaps tried to suggest new ways of communicating, and run onto the hard rocks of confusion and anger, they may opt to look for help, in the hope that a new voice just might offer a new perspective.

Despite coming from different backgrounds, and different theoretical training in counselling/psychotherapy, we are agreed on the value of offering a family space within which each person can freely outline their difficulties in making a decision and be listened to with respect and acceptance. These meetings are designed to help a family find some consensus of purpose, some agreed way forward out of their impasse, and while they can vary in several ways, there are basic commonalities: the time span is short with a once-off meeting of three hours; each family member has the opportunity to give their views on the disagreement, without interruption, without criticism; each person is listened to with respect and, in turn, listens to the others without interruption; solutions or compromises are arrived at by the group, and are not suggested or imposed by the facilitator.

If this sounds simple, on one level it is. It is also profoundly effective, as each family member hears clearly, often for the first time, the opinions and feelings of the others and responds from their own perspective. Given the underlying goodwill, or at least willingness to attend this meeting, the work usually consists of clearing up misunderstandings, re-interpreting entrenched positions and helping people both to clarify their own opinions, and to get a better understanding of the positions of the others. This sharing of knowledge and understanding gives a new awareness of each other, and is likely to result in greater wisdom and a more informed solution or consensus.

In Chapter 1, we outline what we mean when we speak of 'family', as it is not easily defined, and of how it has evolved to become the unit it is today and the characteristics that define it. Chapter 2 describes the meetings we facilitate, how they take place and what transpires as they progress, while Chapter 3 gives a picture of the person of the facilitator, what their work entails within these meetings and how they may influence the group. We then describe four case histories (with names and some defining details changed to protect confidentiality) of families that have participated in such meetings in order to illustrate some of the theoretical statements in the first three chapters.

It is truly astonishing what can transpire in these meetings. The only certainty is that their progress and their outcomes are totally uncertain! One of the families (not included here) fought for at least an hour, until finally the youngest member stated bluntly that he would not speak to the others at home because they spoke to him through the walls. When asked for clarification, he said that they had no respect or consideration for him, because they constantly called out to him from other rooms and would not come and meet his eye when they talked, so he never answered them, and they would get angry. Further discussion around this (which the other family members had not been aware of) revealed that when he was small and came home from school full of information that he needed to share, his mother was always in the kitchen and, although he pulled her skirt, she would never pay him attention or even look at him. He used to feel rejected and ignored, and since then, only when a person made eye contact did he feel appreciated and heard. He admitted that he had always had difficulty using the phone and was astounded to hear that none of the rest of us in the group felt that way. The hard edges of this family appeared to melt and a new understanding enabled new dialogue.

This unexpected twist underlines one of the least acknowledged aspects of our work, which is to truly believe that some form of change is always possible, to share that belief with the group and to ensure that we keep a light of hope alive.

We are aware that each family meeting allows us, as facilitators, to enter into the life of that family, and we have been continually impressed by the generosity of each family that so openly allows us access. This is a privilege rarely afforded to strangers, and we would like to acknowledge it here and hope that we in turn will never use it carelessly or clumsily, but will always endeavour to enhance the understanding and the progress of all the families we work with.

Finding solutions to difficult problems

If we were to choose a motto for this work, it might well be:

> Whatever you say reverberates,
> whatever you don't say speaks for itself.[1]

Note

1   Szymborska, Wislawa, 'Children of Our Age' in *View with a Grain of Sand: Selected Poems*, Faber and Faber, 1996, p. 149.

– 1 –

What is a Family?

Happy families are all alike; every unhappy family
is unhappy in its own way.[1]

Some family dilemmas or disagreements just will not go away.
You or someone you know may have experience of one or all of
the following situations:

* Worrying about an older relative in need of long-term care
* No longer speaking to brothers or sisters
* Having adult children still living at home expecting the same
  service and attention they received as children
* Having difficulty deciding where to spend Christmas because
  wherever you choose will result in rows and disagreements.

Similar difficulties exist in many families because families are
both essential and impossible. At times we threaten to leave
them, to walk away, because despite the inherent closeness of the
relationships, we all appear to speak a different language in times
of stress. And yet within a couple of weeks we are back again!

What is a Family?

> ... families are inescapable ... we carry them in our head.[2]

In his book *Families and How to Survive Them*, John Cleese underlines the poison potential within even the happiest and closest family circle. We so easily hurt one another inadvertently through carelessness and casualness. Sentences frequently begin with 'I thought you meant ...' or 'I thought you were going to ...', and before we know it, we have lost the ability to discuss even a shopping list amicably, and attempts to discuss greater dilemmas are doomed to failure. What can we do? Must we just suffer helplessly or is there a more positive way of communicating without conflict, of solving dilemmas without damaging everyone concerned?

In this book, we will show that there is another way for families to deal with difficult situations and to explore and reach solutions by lessening the potential for hurtful confrontations. We suggest that a once-off meeting of the family concerned, supported by a facilitator and contained by time boundaries, enables each family member to describe a situation as they see it, hear the point of view of others and begin to understand one another and the nature of the basic conflict between them. This new way of communicating can act as a role model and can become the way they speak with one another in the future.

No magic solutions are offered, no quick-fix outcomes are promised, but an attempt to hear and understand each other's point of view, with a sense of safety and suspension of hostilities generated by the presence of a facilitator, will often produce results which are positive, creative and co-operative.

In the ordinary course of events, most of us are part of a family, which itself is situated within society. Many of us also belong to other groups with shared aims, in the workplace or through sport and social activities. We affiliate with and find common cause with others because they have the same interests or they are pursuing a similar agenda, or merely for social company. In order to operate effectively and maintain some form of cohesion to help achieve their agenda, groups usually manage to reach a balanced position where both the interests and wishes of the individuals and the aims of the group can be achieved.

Families are perhaps the most convoluted of all groups and how they work, and why they work in a particular way, is complex and layered. They are different to other social groups because we do not usually choose to be in a particular family. For a family in equilibrium, or 'muddling along', the unique characteristics of the individuals and of the group ebb and flow, and combine to constitute a 'normal' family. If this fragile equilibrium shifts, whether from pressures inside or outside itself, the whole structure may be unsettled and a new balance is sought. 'Like a historic building, the family structure may have been stable for years, but – because it's finely balanced it can still be fragile. As in an old building, individual members have stress points which can cause them, or the family, to collapse under pressure.'[3]

If the disruption is severe, family therapists will work either short or long term with the family and with each of its members. In situations created by a need to make a decision (such as placing an elderly parent in a nursing home), a change in the family structure (a new in-law or the arrival of a baby), an economic upheaval (loss of job or home), the family is not in melt-down but rather unable to cope with present circumstances. We believe that new insights and new coping skills can be sourced from the family group itself during a once-off meeting of all concerned.

The term 'family' can be an overly simple description of a group of people living under one roof – parents and children – with grandparents and extended relations living nearby. World-wide there are different ways of defining a family and in Ireland long ago it was the clan, rather than the family, which defined one's 'belonging'. Families have changed radically. Today there is often only one parent living with the children; often the boyfriend or girlfriend of one of the children will also be living in the family home; a couple (perhaps same-sex) might be fostering a child together.

One of the most efficient ways of looking at, or defining, a family is to see it as a system which will generally tend to move towards growth, despite the counter effects of unfavourable or destructive circumstances that can arise from within or from outside the family. This interdependent organisation is composed of sub-systems of parents, children, grandchildren and so on, and we can focus on the behaviour, interactions and beliefs in all these sub-systems that influence, and are influenced by, all the others. For example, John is bored and annoys his sister, Jill, in order to get attention; Jill nags her Mum to intervene; Mum gets angry with John and reprimands him; John has got the attention he wanted (even though it is negative attention); Dad angrily disagrees with Mum over the parenting issue of how to control the children; now all four members of the family are involved in the interaction, resulting in ongoing and unresolved conflict. This small row illustrates the nature of the relationships between each member of this system and the discord that can arise from even the simplest exchange.

The Family Life Cycle

Composed as they are of individuals, families are also subject to the impact of the major life-cycle stages. An awareness of these normal changes can help identify what is happening for the family, and these can be listed as follows:

- Unattached young adult
- Joining of families through marriage
- Family life with young children
- Family life with adolescents
- Launching children and moving on
- Retirement and old age.

How the individual and the family react to these changes varies considerably. Reaction to unpredictable events such as illness, emigration and accident can cause upset, but when occurring alongside a life-cycle change, the outcome may be considerably greater. (These unexpected events need not all be negative. We have worked with a family that won a large amount of money in the Lotto. This created tensions and secrets for which they finally sought help!) Further stresses such as the drive to attain a higher standard of living or simply inertia about life add further complications to the mix. Reaching any one of these stages may put pressure on the entire family, as the feelings and emotions embedded in the family's history may obscure their present coping skills and their ability to communicate effectively. The combining of more than one stage change for more than one family member can cause even greater confusion and disruption for all.

Family Characteristics

Compared with other groups, families have characteristics that are frequently identified within family dynamics. These inner workings of a family can be determining factors that not only define a family but also influence its interactions and communications. It is relatively simple to list these characteristics (as we do below) and you might recognise some elements that exist within your own family or family of origin. In the case history chapters, we have woven some of these through family stories to illustrate them in a practical way and to show how their destructive potential can be recognised and defused.

These influences do not arise singly or tidily; rather they merge and multiply and are mostly hidden and taken completely for granted. The family members co-exist, at times tolerant, at times intolerant, of one another. It is often only in a crisis that the unseen obstructions manifest themselves and it becomes clear that the family does not have the skills or the knowledge to identify the problems and work around them. What is obvious to an outsider may be quite invisible to those locked within the family defences and boundaries, which may once have been essential to the survival of the family group, but have now become their prison.

Boundaries and Rules

On a street of seemingly identical houses, the boundaries of each define its difference. One house will have a hedged garden to deter balls or animals; the next will have only a soccer net with marked walls; a third may have no front wall in order to facilitate car parking. These boundaries delineate the families that live in the houses in an obvious and external way.

> It is the system's boundary which provides the interface, both with its external environment and with its own sub-systems, and which circumscribes its identity in space and time.[4]

Within each family, parents lay down rules for their children's behaviour, some spoken and many unspoken, outlining the boundaries of behaviour – what is acceptable and what is not acceptable. These boundaries differ for every family, and we can get a very clear picture of how a family works if we become aware of them and the extent to which they are enforced. Explicit rules are much easier to identify – from the practice many years ago that children did not eat meals with the adults in some households, to the rule that children go to bed only when they are tired! Indeed, many families today find it extremely difficult to introduce rules, and even more difficult to maintain them.

Secrets

In the same way as rules are often inherited from the grandparents, or families of origin, and may unknowingly become 'laws' applied without conscious examination, so 'secrets' in the family history may determine how a family operates. We usually experience a secret as something negative that is hidden from one or many by one person or many. In families, however, secrets are often instigated to 'protect' someone, even the whole family, from a perceived threat, real or imaginary. For some families only a few topics are permissible in public or 'outside' the family home, perhaps due to an inherited or inherent fear that they will not be understood or believed.

For others there are subjects that are forbidden both at home and abroad. Children's questions may be fudged or ignored, and the child in turn adopts the habit of not asking about certain topics that may be deemed 'dangerous'. Shame or difficulty explaining an event or experience may be a source of closely held secrets, which can generate powerful alliances between those 'in the know', and thus become weapons in family disputes. For example, a family where there have been adoptions or within which a suicide has occurred may close ranks and shut out the world. Not so long ago, and to a certain extent still today, mental health illnesses such as depression were also taboo.

Secrets can be subversive: they have the power to undermine values or beliefs. In a particular family, there was a belief that anything to do with 'the arts' was highly dangerous. When the underlying secret was finally unveiled, it transpired that Grandma A, who was 'completely off the rails', was a theatre director when she was a newly married woman. As a result, she was never at home – always at rehearsals – to the neglect of her children. The resulting implicit belief was that people connected with the arts were eccentric and never took responsibility within their family.

This secret finally manifested itself when her granddaughter wanted to do a dramatic arts degree and could not understand why her conventional parents objected so vehemently to this course. This family had completely discounted any possible positive value in creativity. The task of the facilitator may thus be to name 'the elephant in the kitchen', the secret which is wielding such power.

Beliefs and Values

The values held by family members are rarely attributable to any specific teaching or discussion, but rather are absorbed by the children as they grow up. As Rudi Dallos says, '... behaviour, beliefs and emotions are linked together so that families attempt to make sense of their world, to ascribe meanings to their own and each other's actions and in doing so construct a repertoire of choices'.[5] Children unconsciously adopt the behaviour of the parents, who are acting out of the beliefs and values they themselves inherited from their own parents. How often do we hear ourselves speak in a certain manner, with definite phrases and inflections, and realise with a shock that this is the voice of our mother, father or older sister! It is often through these verbal belief systems that family members, particularly parents, exert their control over each other and their children.

Parents may have high expectations about maintaining family 'traditions' such as professions, rituals and leisure activities. They may impose and maintain these with statements such as 'our family have always looked after their own' or 'we never throw anything away'. Choosing a family trade or profession because it is what our parents did is traditional. Moral principles and accepted standards of behaviour are also part of our learned inheritance. However, of their nature these are often intangible and elusive, and so it is more difficult to choose them for ourselves.

The impact of these values and beliefs on family discussions can be most divisive, since some family members may be locked permanently into a set of values they never actually chose for themselves, while others may be living their lives in automatic revolt against these same values. Value judgements will be part of all discussion, with claim and counter-claim, challenge and defence blocking any real dialogue. Focusing on belief systems and uncovering them makes us more sensitive to the family's deeply held views and explains both their problems and the language they use to describe them.

Language, Meanings and History

A family will usually hold subjective meanings for many words and phrases, and these 'codes' are often not immediately understandable to outsiders. The mere mention of a well-known family story can send the family off in a particular direction, without having to relate the whole event, and a stranger may be left floundering in confusion because they are not privy to the 'history' of the family. Seemingly casual comments can take on references far beyond the current discussion, and a comment such as 'She's so like her aunt' may be high praise or sad condemnation, but only those within the family group will know.

Language can be used to control: family members may feel oppressed or silenced by the style of language used by others in the family. Many families' relationships function through cohesive language that may achieve the final aim but ultimately may undermine clear and true interaction. In the same way silence can most effectively control or subvert the family members. Because a family has existed over time and therefore has a 'history', this can impact far beyond the literal meaning of words and phrases. Old rivalries may be acted out to the detriment not only of the individuals within the group, but also, more particularly, to the solution of a stated aim or objective. Since the perspective of each family member is different, discussion and suggestions can become both adversarial and personal, resulting in even greater conflict and even wider rifts. The challenge is whether we can compose new endings and outcomes to these scripts written during our childhood.

Hierarchies

Hierarchies exist in all groups, irrespective of the effort participants put into trying to be equal. In rearing their children, many parents take a leadership role, assuming that responsibility for all decision making rests solely with them in the best interests of the children. This is obviously true for very small children. Further, if, for example, the parents' jobs depended on relocation, the decision to move house would not be left to the children, no matter how mature they might be. Hierarchies in the best sense enable parents to be responsible for the general welfare of the individuals and the family as a whole with regard to societal, cultural and emotional beliefs. For a family to function in a healthy manner, a hierarchy is a prerequisite, whether this be both parents equally or one more dominant parent.

What is a Family?

Among the children there will be natural leaders to whom the others look for decision and action; there will be different levels of intellectual and emotional competence. Hierarchies often follow from age levels, as an echo from family tradition, with the eldest being conferred with authority by a parent: 'Look after your little sister while Mam gets the dinner' or 'Listen to her, she's older than you'. Indeed the eldest often actively takes that authority without any adult conferring: 'I'm older and bigger and stronger than you – do as I say!' These patterns can exist for as long as the family survives and are based on 'perceived' knowledge, wisdom or experience.

In Chapter 4, 'The O'Reilly Family', we can see that somehow, sometime in the family history a belief evolved that a hierarchy of power in decision making and control rested with the eldest, Kevin, and this went largely unchallenged. Hierarchies can also be perpetuated by gender, where 'boys are best' and girls have learned to always take second place.

Sadly, unbalanced hierarchies can also exist, for example where one child is favoured and more loved by the parents, while another appears to be almost dispensable. Sometimes a child/children assume a 'parental' role: a daughter can take on the role of 'mother' due to an ill mother. Furthermore, a son can learn from a dominating, bullying father to dominate and bully other family members in turn. In more complex situations a child may be enrolled as 'parent' when a parent abdicates their position, perhaps in order to destabilise or usurp the role of the other violent, abusive parent. There are endless variations that can evolve across generations when that child grows to assume an over-controlling stance with their own children.

As facilitators, we need to be vigilant as to how we approach equality and hierarchy in the family system. While believing that each member of the family has equal status and power, we will acknowledge hierarchical differences, especially generational, within each family.

Locus of Power

Of their very nature, families can encourage the existence of a kind of dictatorship, where great power to affect the family's ordinary living is based within one member or group of members. A need to dominate or become the focus of all family exchanges can have a very powerful impact on how a family operates. We are inclined to think of the decision makers as being either the mother or the father. However, there are times when the decision-making powers lie firmly with the children, who are dictating bedtimes, mealtimes and TV programmes, while the parents appear to be helpless. The tyranny of children can be quite ruthless! It can also happen that a child with special needs requires so much more attention and care than the other children, that family decisions and actions spin around this one person to the neglect of the needs of the rest of the family. This is a particularly difficult situation to cope with, but once it is acknowledged and discussed openly, either the current situation becomes more tolerable or a different way of managing is found.

It is important to remember also that external influences, such as acts of violence by strangers or undue pressure from outside agencies, can powerfully impinge on the family as a whole. The resulting helplessness and dependency on outsiders may further disempower the family unit.

Scapegoating

The powerfulness of these learned characteristics of families can be seen to ugly effect where, for example, family members eager to remove pressure or blame from themselves focus all their ills on a single member. One child, perhaps the least aggressive or the most timid, becomes the source of all a family's misfortunes or problems. Over time, this person often appears to take on this role, actively assigning blame to themselves: 'It must be my fault – it's always my fault – everyone says so.' They may be fearful that, without this role, they will have none, and it lends them a kind of importance, even if it is of a most negative kind.

Changing the Outcome

The communication and feedback mechanisms that stem from these family ways of operating often result in unresolved conflict – unresolved because the family is usually quite unaware of the influence of their past history, and therefore cannot even begin to puzzle out how to change. If this process can be interrupted and highlighted, then the outcome can be both different and positive. In a recent television programme, clinical psychologist David Coleman highlights the effectiveness of working with families where the interaction, and therefore resulting behaviour, of both parents and children are causing major family disruption. Not being historically or emotionally involved with the family members, Coleman can observe the dynamics and suggest ways of changing them to bring about a more harmonious family situation.

In some families, the parents take the unusual step of holding family meetings, even when the children are quite small. The circumstances that require decisions are outlined and the views of the children are sought. Even though the parents make the final decisions, the children feel they are part of a democratic unit; that their views and opinions will be heard and listened to and the reasons for the outcome will be explained to them. This can instil a respect for the ideas and opinions of others and a facility to put their own thoughts into words. (This practice can also result in very unusual meetings. One rule can be that anyone, child or parent, can convene a meeting, on any topic, and some of the resulting discussions have been hilarious!)

For an adult family, intervention by an outside person, as in the once-off meeting we describe, can have a similar effect. This meeting does not attempt to by-pass the potentially destructive elements that can exist within a family and that can manifest whenever the members come together. The facilitator hopes to identify and highlight these elements and, in so doing, lessen their impact in order to focus on the kernel of their current dilemma. Identification is vital, but an in-depth examination of the root causes and an exploration of past history is for future work and family therapy. Such identification and clarification will usually result in some resolution for the family. Solutions are rarely either neat or comprehensive, but the combined wisdom and goodwill of the group can almost always identify a desirable next step. New and creative suggestions appear, which quite often win the approval or acceptance of even the most belligerent and argumentative of the family members!

Notes

1. Tolstoy, Leo, *Anna Karenina*, NY: Barnes and Noble, 1992, p. 3.
2. Asen, Eia, *Family Therapy for Everyone*, UK: BBC Books, 1995, p. 8.
3. Ibid., p. 12
4. Walrond-Skinner, Sue, *Family Therapy: The Treatment of Natural Systems*, UK: Routledge and Kegan Paul, 1997, p. 12.
5. Dallos, Rudi, *Family Belief Systems, Therapy and Change*, UK: Open University Press, 1991, p. 14.

– 2 –

The Family Meeting in Action

[Values] are not carved in stone, but written by a human heart.[1]

As mentioned in Chapter 1, we believe that holding a once-off family meeting with a facilitator can empower a family to source new insights and new coping skills from within the group. The main features of such a meeting are quite specific:

- The meeting takes place within a specified period of time, agreed in advance – currently three hours. This immediately creates the awareness that there will be a focused and limited time for discussion, without the spectre of endless and repetitive conflict.
- The presence of an independent facilitator, who becomes part of the group meeting but who is obviously not part of the family group itself, is a guarantee that the meeting will not be merely a re-hashing of old patterns.
- Within the group, the facilitator becomes a focus point towards whom remarks and explanations can be directed. Point-scoring and derogatory statements can be filtered

through this neutral person, who will clarify and reflect their content without absorbing the emotional hurt or anxiety. In this way, the core of a problem can be tackled, all opinions can be heard without interruption and mutual understanding can be brought closer.

- The actual arrangement and commitment to such a meeting can bring some structure and purpose even before the meeting takes place. A landmark or milestone has been put in place where attention can be focused on the difficulty that confronts the family.

Reasons for Meeting

The purpose of such family meetings is to solve or resolve a disagreement, to find a solution to a shared dilemma through improved communication between the participants. Meeting *specifically* to do this may prevent a serious escalation of conflict. The way forward is not clear, or it may be clear in a different way to each participant and there may be as many suggested solutions as there are people involved. Carl Rogers noted that

> … the major barrier to mutual interpersonal communication is our very natural tendency to judge, to evaluate, to approve or disapprove, the statement of the other person, or the other group … the tendency to make evaluations is common in almost all interchange of language, it is very much heightened in those situations where feelings and emotions are deeply involved.[2]

The presence and participation of the facilitator, who is able to lay aside their own feelings and evaluations, and listen with understanding to each participant, can assist the process of working together. A tired debate or well-worn discussion can be invigorated by the fresh understanding the facilitator brings to the session. By clarifying the views and attitudes each family member holds and by creating space for both speakers and listeners, the facilitator increases the possibility of a shared solution being found.

The difficulties and the pitfalls of communicating within a family can become magnified and exaggerated when a decision or an action needs to be taken. Those very closely involved in a situation tend to lose perspective, and the heightened sense of crisis adds further confusion to their already fraught communication. Attempts to reach agreement through phone calls or over cups of tea may result merely in arguments or angry exchanges. 'I wash my hands of the whole matter', 'Just count me out', 'I don't care, they can do what they like' – these are the kinds of comments that can follow such rows. It is definitely 'time to talk' but in a different setting.

Within many families, the routine of discussion begins with disagreement on trivial matters, but can slip quickly into mutual exchange of hostilities. The presence and independence of a facilitator, who is not carrying their emotional history and baggage, and yet becomes part of the group meeting, is a guarantee that the meeting will not be merely a repetition of familiar statements which lead nowhere.

A third party, who is able to lay aside his own feelings and evaluations, can assist greatly by listening with understanding to each person or group and clarifying the views and attitudes each holds.[3]

When participants pause for long enough to *hear* what the others are trying to say, and to win space to make their own position clear, then the vicious circle can be short-circuited and the potential for a new form of dialogue and communication can result.

Composition of Group

What constitutes one family can be very different from another. Generally, those who come to such a meeting include the family members who are directly involved in the situation for which they seek help, and the invitation to attend comes from the family member who initiates the meeting. In general, we confine attendance to adults or older teenagers, as these are likely to be more conversant with the idea of family on a larger scale than that which merely impacts on themselves. If a particularly large number of family members wishes to participate, for example more than eight or nine people, we would suggest that there be two facilitators present in order to create for all an essentially equal opportunity to participate.

There is no ideal number of participants. The family in this context are all those members either connected directly to the problem or those who wish to have an input and be part of the solution. In general, despite careful booking, there will be family members – sometimes all of them! – who do not come to the meeting. While some of their reasons for non-attendance are genuine, sometimes people just cannot find enough courage or confidence to face what they see as a confrontation. If a particular member of the family refuses to come, or another lives too far away, or the convenor thinks another would not be able to attend, this does not mean that they are not interested. They may be notified of the meeting and of the outcome.

Each family member present will get an opportunity to speak and explain their thinking and feelings around the 'problem', and space will be given to those who find it difficult to ask for or use their time to speak. It can sometimes be interesting to hear who has been omitted, for whatever reason. At times the absent family members appear to wield even more influence than if they were truly present, with participants referring to them, quoting them and feeling fearful of how they will react to whatever decision is taken

Space and Time Boundaries

It is important that meetings take place in a neutral environment, often the facilitator's work space: not too formal or official – a sense of casual comfort is ideal. Neutrality diminishes distractions, providing a safe and contained context. This has numerous advantages. It means that no previous family history is connected to this space, so there are no subliminal associations working either negatively or favourably for some family members. It also allows attention to remain fixed within the group and its discussions – if meetings were held in settings that were familiar to the participants, they could, for example, waste time playing host.

Having a specified period of time helps to maintain focus and creates a delicate sense of urgency. It reminds everyone that there is a limited time for discussion and that this is not the place for engaging in endless and repetitive conflict. This does not necessarily constrain the work, which will be neither hurried nor superficial, and it certainly focuses the collective mind of the group, creating a known and dependably safe closing point for all concerned.

Mid-session Break

Three hours with a break of twenty to thirty minutes seems to meet the requirements of concentration, attention span and physical comfort. It also allows the members to be 'time sensitive', aware both of time elapsed and time remaining, while maintaining their own independence and concentration on the pivotal focus which brought them together. It can release tension, create a respite from intense concentration, be a bathroom opportunity, permit everyone to regain composure and allow dispersal from fixed positions.

This 'time-out' for the family is also particularly important for the facilitator. Within it, they have time to:

- Make a brief assessment of the progress of the session.
- Make a note of unclear topics or views which need further clarification
- Evaluate the extent to which the 'problem' has been given precedence over the family dynamics, and how well the focus is being maintained on this main issue.
- Above all, it gives an opportunity to the facilitator to process, however briefly, their own feelings and emotions, and their

impact on the work, while pausing in the momentary calm of this break.

Getting the Family Conversation Started

The fact that the family members have each made the effort to come to such a meeting suggests a commitment to searching for some resolution to the present dilemma. It is a statement of interest and willingness to be involved and to make a contribution, whether negative or positive. The facilitator's neutrality creates safety, and helps to prevent mere repetition of old conflicts. At the start they outline the problem or dilemma that has brought the family members together, and ask if this is how they all see it. An unacknowledged difference of opinion about the purpose of the meeting could create great confusion. The facilitator may point out that their very presence suggests that they all wish for an agreed outcome and shows a willingness on their part to try to resolve the issue. The initial exchanges can influence the direction of the meeting, so it is important that the facilitator is aware of this, as the following example shows:

> **Facilitator**: 'Mary contacted me initially to request a meeting at which we could discuss where your father will live, as you are selling the family home. Perhaps you could tell me how you each see this decision.'

> **Frank**: 'There is no decision yet! That's just Mary jumping the gun and taking over as usual.'

> **Edward**: 'Rubbish Frank. We all need the money if we're going to look after the old man, and where else do you think we're

going to get it? We've already spoken to the auctioneer, so what are you on about?'

Mary: 'That's right, you two. Turn it into a battlefield and waste all our time. This is discussion time and we've got to look to the future.'

Anne: 'Wouldn't it be great if we won the Lotto. Then we could go on as before and Dad would be fine where he is. We could employ a couple of nurses to look after him in the old house.'

Facilitator: 'I get the sense that none of you are really listening to each other, and that you're trying to reach a solution without really discussing what it is you are trying to resolve. Perhaps you could each tell me the situation as you see it right now.'

The real meeting started at this point. The group began to give shape and substance to the difficulty that had brought them together, without resorting merely to their old ways of communicating. The vicious circle of accusation and counter-accusation had been interrupted and there was now potential for real dialogue and discussion.

The primary reference point for the group is the presenting problem. There is a difficult balancing act between the need to find a solution to this problem and the parallel need to ensure that no individual is sacrificed for the group need. There is a risk that the immediate difficulty would be solved but the family would continue to tear itself apart as before.

Customary Family Interactions

Family members will have evolved automatic ways of responding to each other which will be reflected in this meeting. Well-worn discussion and arguments within a group tend to follow familiar lines. For example, if I have always felt inferior to a more beautiful/more intelligent older sister, and if comparisons voiced by others over the years have confirmed this, then I will almost automatically fall back on childhood reactions when we discuss something serious. If, in the past, I adopted a defensive and jealous way of interacting with this sister, then when we seek solutions to family problems today, it is likely (and understandable) that I take a defensive and jealous stance. My contributions to family discussions will revolve around this accustomed response. Our history echoes through today's exchanges.

'I'm not going to discuss this with you because you always take his side!' 'You always' is an indicating phrase, which is often met with a hot 'No I don't!', which in turn prompts 'Yes you do – you're disagreeing with me again. And stop shouting. I just knew you'd stand up for him'. Whatever message is struggling to be heard here has little hope amid the din of the almost automatic anger evoked. Neither person is listening; both are treading on familiar ground and the door to any real meeting of minds or hearts is locked once again.

It need not be so. If the voice of a third person is included in this well-learned exchange, then this new note can radically alter the tune.

> **A** [*addressing B*]: 'I'm not going to discuss this with you because you always take his side!'

34

Facilitator: 'If I could intervene – you already sound quite angry and I'm wondering why?'

A: 'Because I'm tired of the same old topic with the same old result – nothing!'

Facilitator: 'You'd like something different to happen?'

A: 'Well, yes.'

Facilitator: 'Could you say to me what you would like to see happen?'

This gives B an opportunity to hear an unemotionally charged point of view from A – perhaps for the first time ever – because it is directed towards the facilitator rather than him.

When A responds with her wish for the future, then the facilitator invites B to repeat what he heard A say and outline what he in turn would like to see happen. Some clarity now begins to emerge.

How Meetings Evolve

The only constant about this work is that anything can happen! There are no certainties, and spontaneity and flexibility are the main ingredients. Between ourselves, and especially during the writing of this book, we have discussed many times a range of 'what ifs?' without coming to any satisfactory answers, but with certain knowledge that practically every session will introduce some element that is new and unexpected and at times even bizarre.

- What if a family member who declined to attend were to turn up half-way through the meeting, demanding inclusion?
- What if, during a meeting, one participant were to accuse another of childhood abuse?
- What if several of the participants decided to storm out of the meeting half-way through?
- What if everyone were to freeze and no one was willing to speak to anyone else?

We do not believe that there are universal answers to these questions or that we can anticipate all eventualities. There is nothing formulaic about this work. Our only comfort derives from the phrase 'Trust in the process!', which means that the family will move closer to their own solutions in the course of a meeting. It may be 'good to talk', but much of this value depends on what is said, how it is said and who is listening.

Writing about these meetings, we are aware that capturing meanings and feelings from cold words is far from simple. We have paraphrased what each person said, because these meetings are not recorded, and we have also tried to convey both the feelings and the atmosphere correctly. We have included some of our own reactions and thoughts to reflect our experience of the meetings as we try to remain alert to the underlying feelings, the subscript, as well as to what is not being said and what is being avoided, ignored or actively hidden. So often those involved are failing to connect with each other in 'psychological space', remaining rooted in their own frame of reference.

This meeting does not attempt to by-pass the potentially destructive elements that can exist within a family. Emerging differences are not ignored or papered over; they are safely explored in the space created. The facilitator hopes to identify and highlight these elements and, in so doing, lessen their impact in order to focus on the kernel of their current dilemma. Such conflicts obviously do not disappear but this is not the forum within which to delve deeper. The purpose of this meeting is to seek consensus on the particular problem presented. The acknowledgement and containment of the old conflict is sufficient for now, as the group concentrates on their immediate task of seeking solution to their present dilemma. Future options and contacts for counselling or family therapy can of course be discussed.

For the duration of the session, the focus is on each individual person as they speak, but with an awareness that the person is at the moment part of a group. The facilitator operates from the interspaces between and among the members of the group, creating a focus point within themselves, towards whom remarks and explanations can be directed.

Real communication can take place when we listen with understanding and without judgement, trying 'to see the expressed idea and attitude from the other person's point of view, to sense how it feels to him, to achieve his frame of reference in regard to the thing he is talking about'.[4] As the problem is described from the perspective of all present, with clarification of true meanings and clouded descriptions, a round view of the 'problem' emerges, which all can see, with areas of difference clearly stated.

We should point out that this is how it usually is. There are, however, always exceptions. A family once came together to discuss the sale of their family home that had been in their family for generations. All in their forties, three came from different parts of Ireland and three from abroad. The eldest had organised the meeting, fearful of disagreement, and had made all the arrangements by phone. It transpired that the whole group had not been together since their mother's funeral fourteen years previously. Far from being the abrasive and contentious discussion that the convenor had feared, our meeting evolved into a convivial get-together, with stories and reminiscences exchanged. The decision to sell their home was unanimous and the facilitator felt quite redundant. The most essential thing she had to do that day was to serve them tea!

Outcomes and Solutions

From the real communication engendered in such a meeting, a solution is more likely to be found – and this will come from the participants. The facilitator's work is to highlight the family's historical ways of communicating and differences of interpretation, thus encouraging them to explore both the choices they are aware of and sometimes new options. Often a family will decide to act in a certain way, and agree to sort out the details at a later time. For example, most family members will have a general idea of what is available for care of the elderly. One might suggest a 'home help', another a live-in carer, whilst a third might think day-care facilities would suit best. While it is not our role to identify services, by highlighting and encouraging further research, and encouraging the group to identify their own strengths and resources, we can enable the family to make an informed decision.

The family meeting in action

These outcomes can rarely be foreseen and there are no magic solutions. At the beginning the family may not consciously know where the difficulty lies, so the work consists more of resolution – the act of resolving or of reaching a decision – than just focusing on a specific answer. The solution will eventually be found within the family. The history of the family is deep-rooted and old, but the immediate issue is usually comparatively new or about to happen, and while the difficulties involved may not appear to be immense, they may be daunting to the group members. The thrust within most groups towards creatively resolving each issue, and its potential for solution, points towards a satisfactory outcome. Where this potential for consensus is either unavailable or not strong enough at this time, then a family will find it much harder to find satisfactory outcomes.

Irrespective of their preferences or prejudices, the facilitator, recognising that each family has the *right* to choose their eventual course of action and that members share the responsibility for group decisions, learns to trust the group's ability to change and grow, and supports the group members and their objective. This belief and trust in the process is not intended to suggest that every meeting will result in sunshine and light, but by listening and hearing, by shift and compromise within the held safety exercised by the facilitator, the group will almost invariably work its way towards an agreed outcome.

Notes

1. Rogers, Carl R., *A Way of Being*, NY: Houghton-Mifflin, 1980, p. 195.
2. Rogers, Carl R., *On Becoming a Person*, UK: Constable, 1961/1988, p. 330–1.
3. Ibid., p. 334.
4. Ibid., p. 331–2.

– 3 –

The Facilitator

Others had echoes, gave back your own call
With a clean new music in it.[1]

Can families have this kind of meeting without a facilitator?
Of course they can. Many families have regular sessions of
perhaps an hour, where everyone can ask their question, make
their complaint and feel that they have a voice in how their
family operates. This empowers each adult and each child,
without giving them power over other family members.
Questions can range from asking why they are expected to eat
certain food, to why they cannot go unaccompanied to the
disco, to queries about certain aspects of a parent's behaviour
(difficult!), to giving their opinion about a suggested house
move. Its importance lies in giving each family member a
voice, an opportunity to seek clarification and express
opinions, and, above all, to hear reasons behind rules and
decisions, and to feel they have an input that is treated as
worthy of consideration.

When a family reaches adulthood and the issues become
more complex, having a facilitator can make the process easier,

but what kind of person is this facilitator? Some all-seeing, all-knowing person of power who will draw peace and harmony from some magical therapeutic hat? Obviously training and experience are essential, but basically a facilitator is just what the word says: someone whose presence and interaction with a family makes it easier for the members to discuss, explore and clarify a problem area, and search for, and reach, a solution

Below are some of the positive aspects of the work of a facilitator and some of the attributes and skills that make this achievable. No magic, no power – just someone creating a safety zone and encouraging dialogue.

Self-awareness

A facilitator is a real person in a real relationship with the family. It is essential that they be fully aware of themselves, because issues may arise that have the potential to unleash strong feelings or prejudices within them, which, if not identified and understood, may cloud their ability to recognise them in the family. The facilitator will not carry the emotional history that weighs on the family members, and this neutrality will prevent them from being drawn into the family's games.

The facilitator tries consistently not to involve their own emotions, values or judgements but to bring to the session their skills and personality for the benefit of the group members. They are fully present and responsible to the family, maintaining a balance between the safe space and boundaried time, plus the unknown content and direction. Alert to changing moods and alliances, they remain ready to maintain focus, remind each person why the group has come together and resist being responsible *for* the group and its decisions.

The facilitator's relationship is with the group as a whole, empathising with each family member but entering into alliance with none. No family member is given the opportunity to feel that they have a special relationship with the facilitator, who maintains the same closeness or distance with each family member.

Prejudices

No matter how liberal we think we are, we all prejudge, and almost always negatively. As you will discover in Chapter 5, 'The Nugent Family', the facilitator was initially shocked by the father's apparent lack of care for his Down Syndrome son, and was close to saying 'It is outrageous that you never supported your wife with regard to Brian. How could you get away with that?' To say the least, this approach would have been unhelpful, threatening and quite unprofessional, but from the facilitator's awareness of their own prejudiced reaction, they were able instead to explore with the family the history, meanings and experience around that part of their story to help them find a new way of understanding and relating to Brian. Becoming aware of our prejudices does not eliminate them; rather it enables us to put them to one side and continue to listen without pre-judgement.

The facilitator must also try to be aware of the prejudices of the family group that may be linked to their beliefs and meanings, preventing families from having real and valued relationships. For example, there was an elderly Dublin couple who were having real difficulty adjusting to their new neighbours. For years they had talked over the garden fence with the old couple who had lived next door, but now they were gone and a young family had moved in whom they viewed with great alarm. The facilitator explored the couples' fear, which turned out to be based on a belief that difference equals threat and that *any* change would undermine their security. The new family was being viewed through the distorted lens of old prejudice. (The facilitator, in this instance, had to be alert to their own ambivalence towards newcomers.)

Personality of Facilitator

Whatever the appearance or work style of the facilitator, there are certain attributes essential to their successful interaction with the group. They will need to be interested in each person and somehow convey to each that they are trying to understand and respect their feelings and what they are describing. They will also need to convey their regard for each individual's worth and value, and their concern for each person's welfare, without making this concern dependent on what the person says or does. Finally, perhaps the most powerful lever in this process is the genuineness, honesty and sincerity of the facilitator. These attributes are succinctly and generally known as empathy, non-judgemental positive regard and congruence, and they must not be artificial.[2] They are easy to list, possible to describe clearly, but most difficult to learn and put into practice consistently.

Calm Detachment

The facilitator needs courage and skill to sit with the uncertainties and remain open to the possibilities within the group, and to the variety of human experience. Rich life experience will result in there being less possibility that the facilitator will be shocked or confused. The challenge will be not to try to predict how each family member will react or behave, but how better to understand such reaction or behaviour when it is presented. The facilitator will listen to, and hear, both what is said and what is not being said. Risk is involved for all – the facilitator must rely on their experience of life and their training. The effort not to influence the group by becoming emotionally involved is a delicate balancing act between being real and present, and being professionally detached.

Curiosity

The facilitator's curiosity is a caring eagerness to know and understand more fully the stories and beliefs of the family. It is never merely inquisitiveness or prying. When used as a means to learn more and therefore be more equipped to help, it brings the possibility of hearing beliefs and assumptions in a new way. It is astonishing how people in distress can so clearly differentiate between those who seek information in order to more fully understand and therefore more effectively offer help, and those who seek to know more merely to satisfy their own inquisitiveness. So often the key seems to lie in the way the information is sought. For example, 'Do you hate/greatly dislike your sister? and 'I get the sense that you and your sister have never got on well together': both questions seek information on this particular relationship following on from an exchange of insults, but the latter, gentler, indirect question is more likely to allow exploration without bitterness.

Sense of Humour

> … we all know, from our own lives, that pain may be sometimes unavoidable, it is often easier to be flexible when we are laughing.[3]

If the facilitator takes themselves or their work too seriously, they risk losing perspective and an accurate perception of what transpires when they meet groups at close range. Used appropriately, humour can release tension and can also create and enhance connectedness. Of course if used inappropriately, it can be demeaning and pejorative, disrespectful and wounding. If considered a 'tool', it will alienate the family, but when it springs spontaneously from our true self, it can be most effective and can free a difficult situation to move forward. It is important also to be able to smile at one's own mistakes.

How the Facilitator Interacts with the Family

Not retaining power

So much of society is geared to directing, instructing and controlling – having authority over others because we know what is best for them. This method of working is just the opposite: it accepts the group and each individual member of the group as being autonomous and, further, as being capable of making their own decisions – or at least capable of making their own choice of several different and difficult decisions. The group may wish initially to give this power to the perceived 'expert', out of a sense of defeat or a fear of change, and it is essential that the facilitator resist taking on this power, or attempting to make decisions for the group. It is the group which finds its own solution, decides whether or not to take action and what form such action will take. The facilitator will not abdicate responsibility for their part in what will transpire, but will encourage the group to tap into, discover or rediscover their own power, and make decisions from the strength of this position.

In this brief time span of three hours, the end is present from the very start, so members have their goal and outcome in mind all the way through. Once the family has come to recognise and own its decision-making role, then suggestions and clarifications offered by the facilitator can be filtered by the family, and accepted or rejected. By being willing to suspend evaluation and criticism of the others' point of view, each person comes closer to understanding the position of all the others. The resulting shared perspective of the problem, this new wisdom of the group enables it to reach its own answer through 'a hard-won harmony of all the ideas, needs, and desires of each and every one'.[4]

Effective listening

Listening is all-important and is the foundation on which the entire process – discussion, resolution and outcome – is based.

The facilitator will listen and hear; as a consequence the family members will absorb information. Not only will the facilitator listen to the group as a whole, to the individual who is speaking right now and to the interplay between the members, they will also listen to what is not being said, what is being glossed over or thrown in seemingly as an afterthought.

Experienced listeners will recognise feelings and emotions behind or beneath words and phrases used, of which the speaker themselves may not be fully aware. Just as an oceanographer can look at waves breaking on a beach and be able to read distant seas in the manner and strength of their breaking, so an experienced listener will be able to hear and recognise depths of emotional turmoil beneath calm and seemingly unimportant words.

> When the parties to a dispute realise that they are being understood, that someone sees how the situation seems to them, the statements grow less exaggerated and less defensive ...[5]

Existing hierarchies within the group may be noted, and perhaps sometimes highlighted, but will not be maintained or utilised in the work. The facilitator will always bear in mind that the participants are equals and that their contributions will be considered equally. To ensure that each family member has a position and a voice, the facilitator will try to equalise the space utilised by each person. A partisan facilitator, who appears to take sides or to favour one or other of the group, will not only hinder free expression but might disastrously recreate some facet of earlier family history.

The facilitator

Commonplace phrases and reference points may have very different meanings for a particular family, so listening in these circumstances needs to be particularly acute. Attentive to the possibility that there may be closely held, unmentionable secrets and myths determining the shape of relationships and behaviour within the family, the facilitator will uncover these by saying the unsayable and speaking truth aloud. Their presence can improve both communication and understanding between the members. Because the facilitator does not have their guard up, because they are being real and open, there is less pressure on the family members to dissimulate and they in turn respond without pretence. If the facilitator can show that their only intent is to understand rather than to judge, then the 'defensive distortions' that are causing the conflict can fade away surprisingly quickly and the search for a solution can begin.

> The influence of such an understanding catalyst in the group permits the members to come closer and closer to the objective truth ... mutual communication is established and some type of agreement becomes much more possible.[6]

Thus although emotions may be heightened by a sense of crisis, or by the actual meeting of the different members, and even though there may be an initial reluctance to listen, the presence of a neutral, understanding, empathetic person can counteract this potential emotional explosiveness. 'Misheard misunderstandings' become rarer, and a climate of acceptance and tolerance emerges that is more conducive to problem solving.

The facilitator will listen to the 'expressing' rather than to the 'expression', and will work with the protective layers surrounding each family member. Ideally they will listen while remaining impartial and free of bias. They will try to access the reality beneath each layer, and show that they accept the disguise and the need for it, but that they can also accept what lies underneath. This renders it safe for each person to speak plainly and without guile, without fear of retribution, so '... they can lay aside some of their defences and truly listen to the other person. Often for the first time they begin to understand how the other person feels, and why he feels that way. Thus mutual understanding begins to pervade the interpersonal interaction'.[7]

With this active listening, the facilitator will highlight differences between each member's interpretation of facts or events, and problems will be explained in such a way that no one is blamed or held responsible for disagreements and rows. This strategic reframing by the facilitator alters the family's internal model of the world in relation to the presenting problem. The situation is described and the conflict outlined so that it can be discussed, and hopefully resolved, without further rancour. Acknowledgement and acceptance of the differences between the members – differences of values, goals and methods of achieving these – can help to clear the air. In this new clarity, increased understanding and creative solutions can be discovered.

Validation and positive connotation
The facilitator asks each member in turn to express their views on the relationships and differences between other family members and how they see the problem that brought them

together. They gather further information and introduce new information to the family through a series of listening skills, including tracking and mirroring the language used by the family – different expressions, sayings, tones of voice. They reframe what they hear, thus effecting an alteration in the way it is heard and understood by the others. It is essential to approach all versions of reality offered by family members as equally valid and to accept each person's understanding of their situation, by amplifying and expanding the new patterns that begin to emerge, and encouraging exploration of these.

The facilitator gives value to behaviour that may be regarded by the family as the very problem that brought them together. For example, a truant teenager maintains the parents' focus on him, thereby ensuring that their imminent separation cannot take place. The facilitator might firstly commend the boy for trying so hard to keep his parents together and then invite the family to explore ways of ending the truanting while at the same time addressing their marital relationship difficulties.

Knowing when to intervene – containment and focus

Knowing when it is appropriate to intervene demands experience, intuitive response and courage. A facilitator might intervene from their need to control proceedings or from a wish to protect, or rescue, one of the family members. However, it is essential that their interventions never become mere interruptions. A valid reason is required, such as an effort to maintain focus if the members appear to be veering towards mere gossip or chat, or in an 'I did / you didn't' exchange between two members that is getting out of hand. The facilitator can take the risk of exploring possible but unknown outcomes that may not have surfaced because of fear.

There may be occasions when a family member introduces another issue, which, though relevant to them, may not be pertinent to the presenting problem. They may try to sabotage the session or divert attention from the issue at hand. The facilitator would be wise to intervene and present the group with an immediate choice: do they wish to deal with this new issue or continue to focus on the difficulty which brought them to this meeting, returning at some later time to the now public information. This is the group's choice, which the facilitator is careful not to take from them.

Group Negativity

It is essential to leave room for surprises and to expect the unexpected. Remaining flexible is part of the facilitator's skill, as is accepting the possibility – even the likelihood – of encountering hostility within a group, which can take several forms. Part of the pain experienced when there are family problems is a loss of hope and self-confidence. Some participants may have come reluctantly; their anger may be directed at other family members or occasionally at the facilitator. Dealing with this negativity can be very tiring and difficult at times. It is important to focus on it objectively, because how the facilitator reacts to such challenges can seriously affect the process. It can be a risk to say the unsayable or to focus on what has been glossed-over, but by accepting and acknowledging the anger or resentment, the facilitator ultimately makes the situation safer for all concerned, and can then clarify the feelings behind the hostility. To appear to collude with those who are positively involved in the meeting or to attempt to coax or mollify those who are expressing negativity would probably increase the alienation of the reluctant participants.

Sometimes a family member will challenge or criticise the facilitator. Taking up the challenge can result in a trial of strength, in which there can be no winners, and the losers are both the family members and the facilitator. Equally at times some hostility between group members can threaten to disrupt the group. Once again, it is important not to tidy over the hostility, but to acknowledge it openly.

At one meeting, a very competitive family, whose members appeared to be adept at undermining one another, used smart remarks and a show of knowledge to do so. It appeared to be their way of boosting their own selves by putting the others down, and it was not an admirable way of communicating or interacting. This group started the meeting by setting out to bait or de-skill the facilitator, seeking to catch them out or trick them into a mistake or inaccurate piece of information. This was possibly what they normally did when they felt ill at ease or in some way lesser; it seemed that they disliked having to seek help or advice from a stranger and this was their automatic defence – to undermine and belittle that stranger. It quickly became obvious what was happening. The facilitator responded by bringing to their attention the undermining remarks and discussing them plainly, so that the group recognised what they were doing and why. (A less disruptive challenge might be allowed to pass unheeded, because the time constraint does not permit too long a diversion.) This meeting ended up remarkably successfully.

It is interesting to speculate what might have happened if the facilitator had not had the experience to work with this. The outcome might have been total confusion or open conflict, or even some personal satisfaction for the facilitator in 'winning'. Ultimately, everyone would have lost.

Conclusion

Overall the facilitator needs to have confidence in the effectiveness of this way of working, as well as confidence in their own abilities to help the group. They need to be very clear about their role, remembering all the time that the group has the inherent knowledge and ability to make its own decisions, and that the facilitator's task is to create the climate and setting, and to encourage the communication that will bring about this goal.

After such a session, which dwells on tensions and can sometimes create new ones, counselling/therapy can be beneficial for members on a one-to-one basis. This could help in coping with new family dynamics or coming to terms with an agreed solution. If a member of the group asks for a referral, the facilitator may either offer a selection of suitably qualified counsellors/therapists or supply the name of a professional organisation. It is generally not a good idea to work further with the family ourselves, or with individuals from the group, as this could bring up boundary issues, such as being seen to collude with one family member, thereby precluding any possibility of a follow-up session. It could also create confusion about the perceived role of the facilitator, which is distinct from the role of psychotherapists and counsellors.

Finally, the facilitator is the main custodian of hope in a positive outcome. Knowing and trusting the effectiveness of this one-off session is at least as important as their ability to work in this way: a family despairing of a solution may sense the facilitator's confidence in the possibility of a positive outcome and discover a new-found hope for themselves.

Notes

1. Seamus Heaney, 'Personal Helicon' in *New Selected Poems 1966–1987*, UK: Faber and Faber, p. 9.

2. *Empathy* is the attempt to enter into and to understand another person's world from their viewpoint, without one's own feelings becoming enmeshed with theirs.

   Unconditional positive regard is the acceptance of others as they are, without making this acceptance conditional on how they think or behave.

   Congruence, or genuineness, is the ability to be truly and really oneself, without mask or facade.

3. Jones, Elsa, *Family Systems Therapy: Developments in the Milan-Systemic Therapies*, UK: John Wiley & Sons, 1993, p. 66.

4. Rogers, Carl R., *A Way of Being*, NY: Houghton-Mifflin, 1980, p. 334.

5. Rogers, Carl R., *On Becoming a Person*, UK: Constable, 1961/1988, p. 334.

6. Ibid.

7. Ibid., p. 327.

– 4 –

The O'Reilly Family: Care of the elderly

No man can reveal to you aught but that which already lies half asleep in the dawning of your knowledge.[1]

Introduction

Decisions that may appear clear-cut to one family can bring worry and fear to another. Placing an elderly relative in a nursing home is a familiar situation for many of us today, but this by no means lessens the distress and unhappiness it can bring. There is a finality about it, a sense that it is bringing eventual loss or death a step closer. In some families, it can cause a tearing apart of treasured family values and acceptable behaviour. It can bring a measure of guilt, of betrayal, a feeling of having failed the loved person by handing their care to others. It can also remind us of our own inevitable ageing. For the nursing-home option to become in any way acceptable, sometimes it requires an accident or near-tragedy, such as a fall or a potential fire hazard, which rings alarm bells for all. Add to this the relationships between those who will make the decision, and their connections to the person involved, and it is little wonder that agreement is only reached with much difficulty and heated discussion. With all these complications, potential intrigues and possible flash-points, a three-hour meeting sounds far too brief to come to any satisfactory conclusion. However, this topic has usually been hovering for so long, half-discussed or obliquely referred to, that by the time it is aired at the meeting, it is familiar at least in outline and possibly also in some detail.

Initial Contact

From the initial contact, it sounded as if the O'Reilly family were really in trouble. Speaking to me on the phone to arrange an appointment, Susan's voice wavered and almost broke several times. She had found our leaflet by chance and it seemed to be an answer to prayer. The burden of care for the O'Reilly mother had been on Susan's shoulders for many years and now that she was no longer capable of doing this satisfactorily, her siblings felt aggrieved that they should be disturbed. What was wrong with the current arrangement? Hadn't Susan always been there?

Susan said she was desperate. Her father had died ten years before and she was looking after her mother, living in the family home. Her brothers and sisters did not understand how hard it was and had little sympathy and even less practical help to offer. She mentioned them by name and where they lived, and repeated an obviously well-worn phrase that I thought might be significant: 'None of our relations has ever been in a nursing home.' I tried to take some hasty notes but because she sounded so near to breaking down I didn't want to quiz her on the phone.

It wasn't much to go on, but I hoped they would manage to come to this meeting as agreed. Susan merely told me that they had all consented – some reluctantly – to come and 'talk things over'. As we will see, this family used their three hours to clarify some of the issues and to side-step discussion of many other painful topics.

The First Half of the Meeting

In the event, all five members of the O'Reilly family arrived at the appointed time. I began by introducing myself and explaining that our work would be confidential. I outlined how we would structure the meeting: one and a half hours for general discussion and outline of their difficulty; thirty minutes' break for coffee; and a further hour for evaluation and conclusions.

> **Facilitator:** 'I know from Susan that your mother is growing older and less able to take care of herself. Perhaps you would each like to say how you see this situation.'

I was careful not to mention any need for drastic change, and certainly made no mention of a nursing home.

> **Kevin:** 'I'm the eldest and I live in America. I cannot understand why we are here. Our family has always been able to solve our own problems and not look to strangers for help or solutions.'

This was fighting talk in the circumstances, and I was surprised at the unemotional tone in which it was delivered. It was a proud and independent opening statement, but lacked spontaneity, and I imagined it had been carefully prepared.

The O'Reilly Family: Care of the elderly

Kevin: 'My mother has worked hard all her life and is entitled to live out her days in the family home. I will not tolerate any mention of a retirement home, which is only a fancy name for the old-styled workhouse.'

I noted Kevin's emphasis on '*my*' mother rather than '*our*' mother. He was coming across as being quite pompous and self-regarding. I was finding it difficult to warm to him as he lectured us all, myself included:

Kevin: 'It would be quite beneath my dignity as head of the family to even consider such a move, and my wife fully agrees with me. I do not know what this family is coming to. My mother is able to manage with very little assistance, and that can surely be provided within her own home.'

I hadn't imagined that anyone spoke in this manner outside of old films. Being the eldest was a position that he took very seriously, and his emphasis on the family having always been able to manage without outside assistance struck me as being perhaps one of the family 'rules'. I wondered how the others would respond to this hierarchical stance, or if they had heard it so often that they no longer noticed it!

When Kevin paused, Kathleen took her turn to speak. She spoke in a conciliatory tone:

Kathleen: 'I am the second eldest and, as I live in France, I don't really know much about the scene here. I don't get home often and have to rely on what I hear from the others.'

She did not allude to what Kevin had said, so I assumed that his manner of speech was familiar to his siblings.

> **Kathleen:** 'I'll go along with whatever the others decide. I don't really feel I have any right to make decisions or plans since I'm not living in Ireland, and I haven't been looking after Mama.'

Indeed, while she was at this meeting 'in person', it appeared that she was not interested in taking part to any great extent. She seemed to be completely detached from the proceedings, and went on to speak of her mother as if she was a distant relative towards whom she had no responsibility. She sounded glad to be distant and uninvolved, but some spark of old family involvement flashed out:

> **Kathleen:** 'And anyway, Kevin, talking about the workhouse or the county home is ridiculous, and it's just like you to exaggerate and try to impress and overpower us all. Such nonsense. Nursing homes and retirement homes today, as you well know, are perfectly acceptable places. Just because you're the eldest doesn't mean you're living in the last century.'

Quite an outburst from Kathleen who, as the second eldest, was not going to be overawed by Kevin! She was sufficiently conscious of the old hierarchy to feel the need to overthrow it.

I thanked them both and invited the others to speak. I was interested to see if they would follow in line with seniority, and they dutifully did so. Clodagh was next, dressed in a smart suit, with her hair tied back, very much the businesswoman.

The O'Reilly Family: Care of the elderly

Somewhat to my surprise, she joined in the revolt against Kevin, the eldest and so often the boss:

Clodagh: 'I quite agree with you, Kathleen. You're taking your usual high moral stance, Kevin, telling us all what is right and what we should be feeling and doing. You've been trying to bully us for years, and even now from America you're trying to boss us around. As if you were the only person in this family who knew anything. This whole business with Mother is down to you and your meddling. Though I must say, Susan, if you had warned us all in good time about Mother's health problems, we could have long ago made proper provision and decisions. And informed choices are vital. I should know as a manager for so many years, and running a home and raising my children.

'Some of you don't seem to care and don't want any responsibility – and that means you, Derek and Kathleen. It always comes down to everyone just talking around this kind of thing, and some of us – always the same ones – having to actually DO something. It certainly isn't my fault that we cannot make a decision.'

This was classic talk for a 'middle child' – who has always had to fight for a voice between the 'bigs' and the 'smalls', and has been without a real ally growing up. Clodagh was willing to attack everyone, take no responsibility for events up to now and point out that she was qualified as a 'manager' if they really wanted someone to manage this predicament. But they apparently would have to ask her, and give her decision-making power! I wondered if the group were so accustomed to this kind of behaviour from Clodagh that they would let it pass as 'just Clodagh being Clodagh'. If so, then it would reinforce her feeling of helplessness, non-involvement and not being listened to. Sometimes a family member can be rendered almost invisible to herself and to the others: when she speaks, they politely wait for her to finish and then continue the discussion as if she had never spoken at all.

Derek had been sitting sideways in the group, not looking at the speakers and not looking at me. He looked worn and stressed, somewhat crumpled and as if he lacked sleep.

Derek: 'I don't know why I'm here. I didn't want to come and I'm sorry already that I did. Just the same nag, complain and fight. Where's the point? I just don't have time to spend fretting about Mam. I cannot talk about it at home because Anna (my wife) never got on with Mam anyway, and we've enough on our plate just now. Some of you know how bad my business is at the moment, or maybe you don't and you don't care. I'm barely managing and I can't stand these family rows. Listen to yourselves. They're always the same and then everyone gets mad and goes away until the next one at a funeral or a wedding.

'Just go ahead and put Mam in a home if that's what she needs. Then the house could be sold and we'd all benefit – and, of course, that would pay for the home. Some of you may be sitting pretty in your big houses and fancy cars, but for some of us life is tough.'

The family was using this session to express resentment that seemed to have been brought to a head by the nursing-home dilemma. I was surprised by how little their mother – her health, her fragility, her need for care – actually figured in their discussions. It suggested that she had not played a large part in their lives since they left home, that they had visited little and that now that she needed decisions, it was a nuisance and little else.

We sat in silence for some minutes, and the resentment and anger in the room was tangible. Eventually, I invited Susan to tell us how she viewed the whole matter. After a visible struggle, her words tumbled out as she spoke passionately about her mother. It was as if she had truly heard the others and had been deeply affected by their lack of expressed love or care for their mother, and their apparent inability to think beyond their own needs and comforts.

Susan: 'You don't really care, do you – any of you? You visit when it suits you, when you can fit it in. And she's been lonely all these years, talking about you, sending presents, remembering your children, and getting older and more fretful every day. She wakes up at night to patrol the house in case there are burglars – sometimes even going out in the rain because she thinks she hears noises. She has accused me of planning to leave her and steal her money. The daily minders last only a few weeks before she orders them out. I'm worried all the time, I cannot sleep and I'm afraid that one day I'll come home and find her dead. I just cannot go on.

'She gets so cross when she cannot remember something, and asks the same questions over and over. She says it's like a fog, a grey fog in her head. And when she's not raging, she weeps and that's worse. And she talks of nothing but all of you, all the time.

'I've told each of you, over and over, that she's getting older and frailer and lonelier, but you just will not hear. Kevin, have you not seen how her letters have changed, the writing more spidery, and the same thing over and over? Did you stop to think why that might be, or did you even notice? And you too, Kathleen. She wrote so regularly and it has become so difficult for her.

'But you were her golden family, far away. And Clodagh and Derek – sometimes she used to believe you too were away and wonder when you would be back. I did let you know. Haven't I rung you every week to tell you how she was, but you only responded with your own tales of woe. How money was short, Derek, and how your high-powered business was such hard work, Clodagh. So don't blame me for your not knowing. You just don't care. I sometimes think you'd all be relieved if she died. You haven't tried to cheer her up for years.

'But now she needs more than I can manage. She needs full-time care so she can be safe, eat well and have someone there if she falls. Of course it's terrible to think of her not at home, being minded by strangers, but at least they will be able to look after her. She deserves that at least. So I'm asking you all to forget yourselves for once and look at what she needs. And she needs it now, this week.'

And quiet Susan burst into tears – tears of anger, frustration and exhaustion. Their mother was finally the focus, the centre of our attention, the reason for our being there. There was silence. Not just a pause or a gap in the proceedings, but a weighted and shocked silence which held us all. The only sound in the room was that of Susan's sobs. I sensed that her outburst was out of character, but then realised that perhaps this was her real self, hidden for so long, finally daring to surface. Her brothers and sisters were silenced totally. Susan had done the unthinkable and said the unsayable. Excuses or defences were in short supply.

After several long minutes, I realised, admittedly with some relief, that the clock had dragged itself to 11.30 and that the first part of our session was complete. I suggested that we take our break, that I would have coffee ready in another room and that we would reconvene in thirty minutes. Tensions slackened and the spell was broken. Everyone stood up and began to utter incomprehensible phrases of politeness.

Facilitator's Reflections During the Break

On reflection, I think it was a good decision to take a break at this point, as the first part of the session had come to an end. I hope that I did not merely choose to escape from the almost intolerable tension. This kind of work is filled with such decisions, and while looking back at them is educational and profitable, it is useless to attribute better or best labels to them. To try to gain understanding, even in retrospect, of what prompted us to act in such ways extends our knowledge of ourselves and our motives, but it would be useless indeed to bemoan what we decided.

The break was somewhat strained, with social niceties being observed in an awkward way. I took fifteen minutes to myself to assess what we had learned and how we might best use the remaining hour. This was a family that appeared to have held together for years, with their mother as their only real common link. When they did meet, like now, the old childhood ways of relating were highlighted and they had no substitute learned adult behaviour from which to speak. The constant references to their ages and relative status within the family suggested that there was little real equality – the eldest the most powerful, the youngest almost unheard. Their place within the family defined their importance, and the boundaries thus created appeared to be strong and immutable, and unrecognised.

These divisions coloured their discussions and the way in which they related to one another. However, this meeting was not the place to explore the reasons for these divisions – family therapy would be a more suitable forum for this kind of work. What this meeting was concerned with was recognising such divisions and highlighting them. Hopefully, the meeting would also lead us to honest and frank discussion, and a true hearing of one another's point of view, resulting in an agreed outcome.

Some awareness of a looming separation, a severing of childhood links (which although unhappy were still links) might have been causing them to hesitate before making any decision. They were shying away from the inevitable, but it was up to them to get themselves past this point. I could not force it on them. Not only had I no right to do so, but if I were to try, I felt I would be offering a new obstacle against which they could again rally, and thus prolong the moment of stepping away from childhood. They were beginning to become their own selves rather than clinging to their identity as sons and daughters, brothers and sisters. I would have to be very careful not to impose *my* ideas and solutions on them. As a family unit, it must be their collective solution.

Susan had stepped outside their communication norm, and it was difficult to see how they would, as a family group, cope with this break in custom. They might go along with the shock and each might speak truth and reality; they might close up and reject Susan; they might cobble together a decision that would allow them to escape from this unknown. Of course, they might choose some path of which I could have no inkling. It would be interesting to see what transpired.

The Second Half of the Meeting

When we reconvened, I reminded the group that we had one hour left and that the purpose of the meeting had been to come to some decision regarding their mother's future and well-being. The group was wary. I got the sense that a scene having been created, they weren't sure would this continue or demand something of them. Their social control had been breached, by one of their own, and they did not know how to retrieve it. The discussion so far appeared to have questioned their very identity as a family and I wondered what would happen next.

Their collective embarrassment was still palpable, but they appeared to have been somewhat touched, because each member of the group now attempted to connect with Susan. While they were in the main not willing to take blame, they did try to convey that they had heard her and were willing to take some action. After much hesitation and throat-clearing, again it was Kevin who undertook to speak first, still sounding both eldest and somewhat pompous:

Kevin: 'I'm glad we've had this opportunity to hear from you, Susan, about how it has been for some time. I'd also like to say that I regret it has been so difficult for you of late.'

I felt this was not easy for him because he did not appear accustomed to making apologies, but he could not resist adding:

Kevin: 'I still think you could have alerted us all sooner, and in light of what you say, I feel that choosing a good retirement home is probably the best we can do right now. I propose that we make no decisions just yet about selling the old house. That can wait until we see what our financial requirements will be and what expenditure will be demanded, and I will do whatever I can there.'

It was interesting to see that this was addressed to me rather than to his siblings. He spoke of the practicalities of nursing homes and medical input and financial decisions. It was as if a tacit decision had been reached that nursing care in a retirement home was the way to go.

Once again they fell into their family position to reply:

Kathleen: 'Oh I agree, Kevin. It does seem for the best. I'll try to get home more often to see what I can do to help. The children are older now and it will be easier to get away.'

I could hear the relief in her voice. There wasn't going to be an explosion after all, and agreement was in sight. Although she had appeared to be conciliatory before all else, she was also concerned at the level of unhappiness of both Susan and of her mother which had been uncovered, and it was she who had hurried to hug Susan and reassure her when she wept as we broke for coffee. Clodagh appeared to be still angry and willing to be confrontative, but as Kevin had shifted his stance, she appeared to be uncertain with whom to do battle. She chose the unknown element, the stranger, myself:

> **Clodagh:** 'Well, I must say, if that has been so easily settled, I don't know why we bothered to come here. And indeed *[directly to facilitator]* you've said precious little. I could have managed just as well if we'd met in my house, and we could have saved ourselves time and money. You have a cushy number!'

Before I had time to even consider responding, Derek intervened:

> **Derek:** 'Shut up, Clodagh. You know well we were rightly stuck and nothing was going to happen. If you could have solved it, why didn't you? Even I can see it's not about "managing" and we needed to hear ourselves in a neutral setting. I'll go along with whatever you all choose, because I do see something has to change. Mam deserves to feel safe and minded. She did it for us all when we were little and it's her turn now. I know I haven't much to offer and I'm really strapped right now, but I'll honestly try to do something to help. I didn't know, Sue.'

This was a real turn around for Derek. His focus had broadened, for the moment at least, to include his mother and Susan, along with his own worries. It might not last, but for the moment he was really a member of this family. Clodagh did not respond to him. I got the sense that she was truly shocked at 'little Derek' daring to answer back and being willing to tell her off, but neither had she actually opposed the idea of a nursing home. Everyone looked at Susan, who had retreated behind a veil of stillness and quietness, which I guessed was her usual family 'disguise'. The others suddenly all looked larger than her, but she spoke up:

> **Susan:** 'I'm glad you all seem to agree what's best for Mam, and I'm sorry if I didn't get across to you before how bad things have become. I'm sorry too for making a scene, but I'm a bit short of sleep. I'll get a list of a few nursing homes that might be suitable and prices, and I'll send them out to you all. I'd really like for this to happen sooner rather than later. It's badly needed now.'

I had some sense that further discussion of the 'problem' had been sidestepped. By focusing on the interplay between them, the indecision had been cleared away. I had got a glimpse of how they were as a family, at least on the surface, urbane and civilised.

The curtain had been replaced, and cold truths need not be spoken aloud again. I mentioned this possibility in my summary to them, and it was politely received but not discussed. I also suggested that they might place a deadline on coming to some decision, given the crisis nature of the difficulty that had brought them together, and they agreed to the first day of the next month as their decision time. And that was that.

Conclusion

Did our meeting help? Usually a group presents for help when all else has failed, so it is difficult to guess what might have occurred had they not come. How did our meeting colour future decisions and actions? Sometimes this is comparatively clear, but not always. What did they eventually decide? Had they shifted to a new family space? Had the hierarchy changed? I believe there had been a change, although whether just for this problem or on a broader level I could not know.

This family group had agreed to come for one session in response to a plea from Susan, the youngest sibling. I was given to understand that they were reluctant to attend. This is quite a common and understandable reaction to such a meeting arranged by just one person: while the purpose is known, the form and content is unknown and therefore may be frightening and somewhat threatening.

There were many stresses and strains showing up in this family, but we did not spend time exploring old conflicts. We mention these as blocks to good and effective dialogue, and then try to improve the ensuing communication. Such conflicts obviously do not disappear but this is not the forum within which to delve deeper. The purpose of this meeting is to seek consensus for the particular problem presented, and this is the primary reference point for the group. I did hope that once the hierarchical controls had been recognised, then a possible new way of relating had been glimpsed and acknowledged as attainable again if desired.

The difficult balancing point is between recognising and discussing the problem and the parallel necessity of ensuring that no individual is sacrificed on the altar of the group need. One of the risks is that the immediate obstacle would be removed, but a family would continue to tear itself apart as before. Acknowledgement and containment of the old conflict is sufficient for now, and future options for counselling or family therapy can be offered or suggested. There are always questions remaining and the answers blow somewhere on a distant wind.

Note

1.   Gibran, Kahlil, *The Prophet*, UK: Heinemann, 1926/1924, p. 102.

– 5 –

The Nugent Family:
Taboo truths

You have been told that, even like a chain, you are
as weak as your weakest link. This is but half the
truth. You are also as strong as your strongest link.[1]

Introduction

The Nugents illustrate how discussion of some events may be
taboo in families. Initially such conversations may be avoided as
a means of lessening the pain, shame or guilt that their exposure
might cause. These taboos are often imposed unwittingly, when
family members are fearful of the outcome, should the secret
come to light. Over time these issues may lose their potency,
becoming just a faint memory, or, as in the Nugent family,
become layered in a complex web of avoidances. Sometimes, the
word 'secret' does not apply and a more useful way would be to
describe them as events or emotional experiences that, at the
time of their occurrence, the person or family did not have the
resources to solve. It is then that they become buried in the daily
life of the family, but when a present issue highlights the
historical difficulty, some family members may feel
overwhelmed. Not only are they responding to the current

problem but they are also faced with the taboos that are linked to it. The problem can become a weak link, exposing a chain of experiences that have the potential to unravel or break a family in crisis. (Conversely, the connections of love and support are the links that hold the family together.)

Initital Contact

Two incoherent voice messages were left on my answering machine within an hour of each other. About a day later the same caller phoned asking for information about a meeting. She said her name was Angela and that she had phoned the day before leaving two messages and wondered why I hadn't replied to her calls. (She had left no phone number.) This time she sounded a bit more coherent, but she was speaking as if all her words ran together. I was really concerned that I would miss what she was saying and I asked her to speak more slowly, saying that the line seemed rather faint.

It was a very difficult conversation but it transpired that she, her husband, their two children and one grandchild wanted a meeting as soon as possible. I offered her a number of different appointments and we agreed a time, but then she went over all the options again and chose an alternative day and time. I felt exhausted and still had no idea what was causing her concern. I tried to give her some further details and information about the meeting, including fee, confidentiality and format, but I was cut off in mid-flow without even getting her phone number or address.

I felt bewildered and as if I had had no control over any part of what had been quite a chaotic conversation. To judge by her speech, Angela either had difficulties in communicating or lived life at such a fast pace that language became speeded up in the process. It was difficult to tell and I didn't want to allow my prejudices (such as imagining that she was incapacitated and therefore unable to make clear decisions) to get in the way of helping this family. The next day a brief message on my answering machine from Angela informed me that another child of hers, Brian, would also be attending. Nothing more!

The First Half of the Meeting

Ten days later, at the appointed time, the Nugent family arrived. When I had ushered them into the consulting room, Angela introduced me to her family at breakneck speed: her husband, Thomas, their daughters, Orla and Aoife, and Orla's son, Linus. The sixth member was briefly indicated as Brian, with no attribution, just Brian. Brian was walking around the room, minutely inspecting pictures on the walls and ornaments on the mantelpiece, while Aoife and Angela unsuccessfully tried to get him to sit down. Linus sat beside his grandfather, head down in his hands, and Thomas looked out the window at the cranes on the building site across the street. Orla sat slightly apart and turned away from the other chairs, tears glistening in her eyes.

I had no idea what was going on. The family had little connectedness either to me or to the room, and when I asked who would like to give me an outline of what the problem was that had brought them here today, silence prevailed. I waited. Brian fidgeted ceaselessly. All the others had their heads down. How different the atmosphere was from the frenetic telephone conversation I had had with Angela and the arrival of the family minutes earlier. However, this was not a serene kind of quiet – it felt more like stifled chaos.

Since no one appeared willing to take the first step, I said I sensed their willingness to attend but that they appeared to be stuck as to how to proceed. I suggested that it might be helpful if each of them were to think about how they, particularly, viewed the problem and how they thought this meeting would help. Finally Orla spoke:

Orla: 'What did Mam tell you about the family on the phone?'

Facilitator: 'Your mother requested a session for the family and that was all.'

Orla: 'Well … Mam and Dad live in our family home in Dublin where we were all raised, and I live there too with Linus. Aoife lives with her partner, Paul, in a flat nearby.'

I thanked her for this factual information and asked whether anyone wanted to add to what Orla had said.

Aoife: 'Paul and I are getting married this year and are planning to move down the country.'

Then there was more silence with all heads bowed except for Brian, who stood up and walked over to Angela, standing close beside her.

Although I now had some basic information, I felt nowhere nearer 'the problem/s'. It was as if there was an invisible object in the middle of the room and this was blocking all communication. I began to wonder if this meeting would go anywhere. I could see clearly that Brian was Down Syndrome, yet nobody had referred to his condition, and he had not even been included in the detail of where they all lived. Was he the immovable object taking centre stage or were there other issues?

I was aware that so far only 'safe' information had been disclosed. Linus, a tall, athletic-looking boy in his mid-teens, was the next to speak, gently and clearly:

Linus: 'Mum and I have lived with Granddad and Grandma since Dad and Mum separated when I was five. Granddad is more like my Dad. I never see my own Dad now that he lives in America. Granddad goes to all my football matches and even takes me to Croke Park whenever he can get tickets. Sometimes I overhear Aoife and my Mum discussing what is going to happen to Granddad and Grandma now that Brian is eighteen and an adult and I don't know what that is about. Also, I know that Grandad will retire next year and I wonder if that is a worry. Another time I heard them having a row about my Mum and me living off our grandparents. I was very upset because I don't want to live anywhere else. Anyway, I often see my Mum giving Grandma a hand when she comes home from work.'

Brian was becoming agitated and quietly Angela had signalled to Orla, who had been sitting beside her, to swap places with Brian. Angela finally spoke, directly to me:

Angela: 'I heard what you said at the beginning of the session about explaining how we each view the present situation. Brian was born twenty years after Aoife. I never imagined having any more children after the girls were born. I went back to work, which I loved, when the children were in secondary school. Thomas and I saved money to help the girls go to university.'

She began to speak faster and faster, like she had on the phone. I had to find a way of slowing her down. It was as if what she was about to say was so difficult or painful that getting it over and done with quickly would make it go away.

> **Facilitator:** 'I realise how difficult it is to talk about these problems, but I really want to hear and understand what you have to tell us.'

Angela burst into tears, sobbing into her hands. Brian leant against her putting his arm around her shoulders. Thomas looked very troubled and asked her to stop crying, saying 'that won't help anything', but she continued to cry for some time. Gradually the sobs subsided and while her family sat around in awkward suspense, Angela falteringly continued with her story.

> **Angela:** 'But when Brian was born I had to stay at home. Thomas couldn't face up to what was required and I felt very much on my own. We couldn't go out much together and Thomas seemed to be out all the time. Even though the girls helped out as much as they could, they were at college, studying and all, and I felt I had no support. At times I felt I just couldn't go on, and whenever I tried to explain this to Thomas, he just wasn't able to talk about it. I felt that I no longer had a life, and though I think he also felt guilty about not pulling his weight,

part of me envied and resented his freedom to just go on with his own life.

'Aoife and Orla went to college and now have good jobs and I'm very proud of them. Recently they have begun talking to me about "getting out of the house more", and although I long for that, I would never abandon Brian. In the past month, Orla has started making enquiries about sheltered housing for Brian. I don't know why, but that is really upsetting me.'

Orla [*defensively, as if in response to an accusation*]: 'I never "interfere" in Mam and Dad's arrangements.'

Aoife [*interrupting*]: 'Well, I don't know about that! You were very quick off the mark to get on Dad's side and get him to support your decision to move back home when you and Pat separated. I wonder how much say Mam had about that!'

Orla: 'Are you still on about that? I must say I thought we'd discussed that to death. You'll be glad to move and get away from us all.'

Aoife: 'And I bet you'll be glad to see the back of us.'

It was like listening to two small girls exchanging well-worn insults in what sounded like a familiar dialogue. I wondered if this kind of exchange had proved a useful distraction in the past from harsh realities, such as what to do about Brian's future. This argument had followed on smoothly from the words 'sheltered housing'.

As if she had not even been listening to the girls, Angela suddenly turned to Thomas:

Angela: 'You're very quiet Tom. What do you really think?'

The abruptness of the question took Thomas by surprise. He pushed his chair back, as if to move away from the family. He seemed even more troubled and uneasy, but eventually he said in a very quiet voice, looking at his grandson, Linus:

Thomas: 'I always wanted a son ...'

And he broke off, close to tears himself. Angela began to cry again; Brian was looking at each family member in utter bewilderment; and the rest of the group gazed at the floor apparently gripped by great embarrassment, but also with some element of fear of what might transpire. I realised that there were many more issues than I had imagined, including Brian's future, the close bond between Thomas and his grandson and what might become of it, the retirement years for Thomas and Angela, Orla's status in the family home and who knew what else. I suggested that this would be a good moment to take a break. Perhaps this was somewhat sudden, but I myself needed to clarify my thoughts.

Facilitator's Reflections During the Break

While the family members had coffee and used the garden for a breath of fresh air or to have a cigarette, I reviewed the first half of the session. I realised how ill-prepared I had been as a result of not being able, during my phone conversation with Angela, to gather any information whatsoever – not even a vague idea of the issues involved or who would be attending. I had no idea to what extent Brian was affected by Down Syndrome and I wondered how much of the discussion he was absorbing.

Most of all, I realised how overwhelmed I had felt by Brian's silent presence. No one had referred to his condition although it was so apparent. Physically, he was very large, perhaps seventeen or eighteen stone. When he had first entered the room he had walked from one painting to another and when he had picked up some of the ornaments on the mantelpiece, I was anxious he might drop one. (And yet I was also aware that he was the only one making some connection to the present.) Linus, by contrast, was a fit-looking teenager, well able to articulate his thoughts. I wondered what it was like for Thomas, Angela and the rest of the family to have Brian amongst them. If *I* felt that he had power to determine their lives, what must it have been like for them? Furthermore, what powerlessness also existed – and for whom? And what about Brian himself?

Relationships between the family members were obviously under strain. What was the implication for Orla of the close relationship between her father and her son, or the impact on Aoife with her sister's status perhaps enhanced by Thomas' love for Linus, and was she jealous? The two daughters were in their late thirties, but there was only one grandchild. Was Angela perhaps torn between her resentment that Thomas had not been more involved when Brian was growing up and her awareness of this current focus on her grandchild? Future changes loomed with Aoife moving, Thomas about to retire, Angela's future dependent on whether or not to give her son into the care of others, and Orla perhaps becoming more responsible for her parents with Aoife living further away.

I was quite confused by all the issues that had been voiced and found it difficult to know which most needed attention. I thought it best to leave this decision to the family themselves.

The Second Half of the Meeting

After the half-hour tea break, I called the family back into the consulting room and they resumed their original seating places. I asked them if they had anything they would like me to know that may not have been brought up so far. Aoife had clearly been crying during the break.

> **Aoife:** 'I want you to know something that is never talked about but is so relevant to our meeting here. When I was twenty years old and at college I became pregnant.'

I glanced around the family to see how this piece of news was being received, but all heads were again deeply bowed, no eye contact anywhere.

> **Aoife:** 'I was about six months pregnant when Mam told us that she, too, was pregnant. We were all in shock. The following months were terrible for us all. I was at college and in my final year. The father of my baby refused to take any responsibility for the pregnancy, except to encourage me to have an abortion, which I absolutely refused to do. That was the end of our relationship. Mam had said she would look after my baby while I finished my studies but when my Una was born, Brian was on the way. Everything changed.'

Here Aoife cried profusely, while the rest of the group looked sad and ashamed. When she could, Aoife resumed her story:

Aoife: 'I felt obliged to give Una up for adoption, as there was no way I could manage to rear her in the house when Mam and Dad had their hands full with Brian. Brian was often sick and in hospital during those early years. Having Una adopted was heartbreaking. None of the family really wanted me to give her away but we just couldn't see any other way out. I feel as if a similar situation is happening now.'

Heads popped up all around with looks of astonishment on their faces. I asked the group if any of them agreed with Aoife and there were silent nods. I also asked the family if they felt the same as Aoife and if I was right in my understanding that they all remembered the heartache of giving up Una and now feared the same misery might result from making a decision about Brian's future. Nods of agreement all round and, in a very fast voice, which I was just able to pick up, Angela spoke again:

Angela: 'Sometimes you have to make hard decisions and just hope they will be for the best.'

I allowed the silence to remain, as I, along with the family, digested the meaning of this story for us all. I was silenced, too, by the enormous sacrifices the Nugents had had to make all those years ago. They had had to choose between Una and Brian. I realised for Thomas how important it was for him to have Linus to love and parent in the way he had never been able to with his real son, Brian. I wondered what life must have been like for the Nugents before the births of Una and Brian. Then another bombshell.

Orla *[gently and hesitatingly]*: 'Linus and myself will move out.'

Angela *[with a determined look on her face]*: 'We are *not* going to make the same mistake twice. That is why I planned this meeting. We have got to be able to talk about all of the things that have happened. We have to stop being ashamed of decisions we made, ashamed of who we give our love to, ashamed of not being perfect. We are not going to let go of what we have got. I love all my children equally. I know I have to take Brian's part. I don't expect you girls to have to. I came to terms long ago with you, Thomas, finding your son such a handful but, like I said, we have all together got to find a way forward.'

Thomas *[looking straight at his wife]*: 'Angela, I wish I had known all along that you had understood my guilt about Brian. I've always felt I left you with such a burden and then when Orla's marriage broke down and she had nowhere to go with young Linus, I saw a new world opening up. I feel bad that maybe unknowingly I have been pressuring Orla to stay here with Linus when, perhaps, she really does want to move out and have her own life separate from us.'

The session was coming to an end. So many issues had been aired, all of which were connected. I asked the family to outline which they thought was the most important issue and what they would like for the future.

Thomas: 'The most important issue is Brian's future. I hope we will be able to prepare him for eventually living in sheltered housing, hopefully nearby so that we can see him often.'

Angela *[looking to Thomas in response]*: 'In my heart, I know it would be best for Brian to have a life of more independence. I do often think and worry about the time when you and I will no longer be able to look after him.'

Orla: 'Yes, I have wanted to have a place of our own but I have never lived alone and am scared of being lonely in a flat, especially now that Linus is growing up and will want to go his own way one of these days. Mam and I are very close and I like to think that we support each other. Sometimes I think we are more like sisters.'

Aoife: 'I want Mam and Dad to have a life. When I was young, I used to be so angry all the time and I resented them and their authority. Now that I am older and have a wonderful relationship with Paul, I see how important it is for Mam and Dad to start enjoying life, to be able to go on holidays. I don't believe that Mam will be able to let go of Brian and I hope that Dad will be just a bit more supportive to Mam. In my heart, I don't believe much will change until Linus grows up. I think it will be very hard for him to leave home so long as Dad has such a close connection with him and a real need for him.'

Here we were, at the end of the session, and Brian had not said a word. I asked him if he would like to say anything. I had no idea what he might say. The family looked at me in astonishment. He, too, looked at me in surprise. I wondered if his opinion was ever asked, even though he seemed to hold such immense power and control over the family's outcome. He stood up and walked around the room a couple of times. He stopped beside Linus and put his arm around his shoulders.

Brian: 'He is my brother.'

Usually part of the role of a facilitator is to sum up at the end of the session, but at that moment I felt unable to do this. I felt exhausted by the intensity of emotion in the room. No wonder Angela used the simple device of skimming across her speech. It enabled her not to have to face, or to cover up, the consequences of choices and events of many years ago. Yet her strength as a parent in holding her family together through so many difficulties was not in doubt. They had not discussed the irretrievable loss of baby Una, and not one member of the family had spoken out and named the pain and hardship of having Brian as a son/brother. Silently, and unintentionally, he had ruled the family by preventing them from making the choices and decisions that they would have wished. The girls had almost left home when he was born, although admittedly they were young adults at the point of becoming independent. Except for the fact that Orla had had to return to the family home when her marriage ended, Thomas and Angela would have been on their own taking care of Brian. All had become so interdependent that there seemed little room for change. And, yet here they were together, although no changes for the future had been decided. The session was primarily an opportunity for all the members to have their say, in a safe context. I became aware that all the family were looking to me, waiting for my comments, so I tried to outline what I had heard about each family member.

Facilitator: 'I am aware, Angela, of your love for your entire family, and of your courage in wanting a session such as we have just had. I realise how difficult it is for you to imagine a different future for yourself and Thomas. I think that the relationship between Thomas and Linus has been an enriching one and mutually important. You, Thomas, have been able to be a "father to a son", with Linus fulfilling some of the dreams you held of having a "son" with whom you could share so many interests.

'I imagine, Orla and Aoife, your childhood must have been very different to this, and I wonder how it was for you to experience your parents so consumed with looking after Brian. As so much has been said and shared in this session, I am sure that you will find a way of having the necessary conversations to make whatever changes you want. It is often the first ground-breaking conversation that is the hardest to have. Not only have you not unravelled, you have shown so much care and consideration for each other.'

Thomas: 'Thank you. We all got a lot off our chests.'

Angela: 'I hope a bit more than just that was achieved.'

Brian walked over to stand beside Linus again. The girls got up and gathered their belongings with a slight acknowledging nod in my direction. Then they all began to leave. Thomas stayed behind to pay the bill with a hopeful look on his face and then he too was gone.

Conclusion

Families are usually aware that there is a problem and often several issues. They hope, just as I do, that they will leave with some sense of resolution, or at least a belief that there can be change. Throughout this session it became clear that there was no easily identifiable issue to be solved, but many painful historical memories had been shared that were less likely to have been unearthed at home. On reflection I had a sense that, intentionally or otherwise, Angela had used this meeting as a rallying call to her family to meet these new circumstances together, as a unit, rather than as a collection of individuals as before. But perhaps this is fanciful. If I had had more information about the family before the session, would I have agreed to see them or might I have suggested couple counselling for Thomas and Angela about Brian?

Six weeks later Thomas phoned. He said everything was much the same except that he and Angela were considering attending counselling together to discuss their relationship and that Angela was in negotiations with the Social Services about Brian's future.

Note

1. Gibran, Kahlil, *The Prophet*, UK: Heinemann, 1926/1924, p. 102.

– 6 –

The Brown Family: Family legacies

Roaming, I am listening still,
Bending, listening overlong,
In my soul a steadier will,
In my heart a newer song.[1]

Introduction

Family legacies are very powerful – not 'the piece of china in the
will' variety, but the legacy of a particular way of being for a
particular family. Reactions and responses to events, as well as
the rules of everyday behaviour, are unique to the family and can
become almost immutable. As if set in stone, it can become
almost impossible for family members to deviate from this
particular path which governs their thoughts and actions.
Working with families that are firmly, and apparently willingly,
stuck in such rules can be very challenging. Firstly, the facilitator
has to become aware of these inherited rules, usually from
statements such as: 'We have always gone on holidays to the
West', with the implication that to do differently would be
unthinkable; or 'We never eat out', with an echoed message, 'We
don't have to because we eat so well at home'! Such statements

are usually made without emphasis, because 'everyone knows that', and they usually contain ideas of totality: everyone, always, never. It is profitable to recognise and query these 'totality' remarks: 'I hear you say you "NEVER" do this and I'm wondering what decides you? Do you think it's not acceptable or just not a good idea?' Asking if they have made a decision about something, instead of having blindly accepted the well-worn statement, can be an important turning point. Alternative decisions can be at least considered and perhaps acted upon, rather than taking an action because it is what we always did. The familiar is no longer the automatic reaction.

Initial Contact

None of this was apparent in the initial phone call I received from Stephen. He wasn't exactly sure what our work consisted of and wasn't even sure if he needed help at all. I asked him to give a brief outline of the problem and he explained that at his mother's birthday party a few weeks before, there was an enormous row, completely out of character for his family. He said, 'It just blew up out of nowhere when I mentioned selling the house'. He went completely quiet on the phone, seconds dragged by. Eventually I said, 'You seem to be very upset, Stephen'. He could barely answer but muttered: 'We're falling apart and everyone says I'm making a mountain out of a molehill. We've always got on well together, and we never fight, but we don't seem to be able to talk about anything important. I don't know what to do, and my wife says maybe we need help dealing with it. We've barely spoken since the party row. Do you think you might be able to do anything?'

I gave Stephen some information about the way we work and told him that I did think a meeting could be beneficial. I asked him who he thought might come to such a meeting and he said his parents would probably attend 'to keep him happy'. His older sister, Rosie, who lives with her teenage son, Cian, in the West of Ireland, would come reluctantly. He felt his younger sister, Trish, who lives with her parents, would definitely be there, as she had already said they needed help of some kind. (He confided that she had mentioned counselling or therapy, but he felt this was 'a bit much'.) Stephen himself was already looking forward to it, but although he was married with two children, he did not think his wife, Gemma, would come: 'The row was really just between my parents, my sisters and myself.' We ended the conversation by arranging a date for the family meeting in two weeks time.

The First Half of the Meeting

We all met two weeks later. The parents, Alan and Betty, sat very close to each other, and Rosie had come with her son, Cian. Stephen and Trish arrived together about ten minutes later, saying they had got caught in heavy traffic. Immediately Rosie said:

> 'If I can be on time coming all the way from Achill, I don't understand why you two have to be late.'

> **Stephen** [*looking pointedly at Cian*]: 'Gemma isn't coming because we thought that it was really just close family.'

For a family that 'never fight' they seemed about to make up for lost time. Tension was already beginning to run high and the meeting had not even formally begun. I introduced myself and explained how the meeting would proceed, how we would structure our time and that our discussion would be confidential. I began by asking the parents, Alan and Betty, to tell me what had happened at the birthday party. Alan spoke first.

> **Alan:** 'I must say I thought it was very bad timing on Stephen's part to bring up the idea of us selling our house at the party. I think he asked Betty were we really going to live out our days in this massive house when there were only three of us in it. Imagine! Just after she'd blown out the candles on her cake. I remember noticing the look of utter shock on Betty's face, and I couldn't believe it when he went on to say that if we sold our house now, with the market so suitable for profitable down-sizing, the extra cash could be invested in the business. That was the end of the celebrating, I can tell you. To frighten his mother like that. It's the one thing I've always tried to be firm about. Betty is easily upset and I wont have it.'

It did sound quite shocking to me too, picturing the happy scene and the resounding silence after such a query. But Alan sounded merely irritated, rather than extremely angry.

> **Betty:** 'I really cannot imagine what got into him. Everyone knows how important my home is to me and I'm always saying I'll only leave in a box. How could he even suggest such a thing? But then again, why am I surprised? Stephen has never had any tact.'

Like Alan, Betty was not angry, merely somewhat annoyed at Stephen's suggestion. Was I over-reacting and expecting these people to respond and feel as I imagined I would have done? This is an ever-present danger in this kind of work, and I needed to put aside any focus on my own potential reactions. I did not yet have a clear picture of this family and how they interacted.

Stephen: 'For God's sake, I was only making conversation. It was a birthday, we were talking about ages, and it seemed quite ordinary to move on to what's going to happen shortly when you retire and I take over the business. You know it needs capital, Dad, to expand, and it either grows or goes under.'

Alan: 'I get nervous when you talk so easily of expansion. This Celtic Tiger won't last forever you know, and borrowing money is always unwise. You'll make your mother unhappy like you've done so often before.'

Stephen: 'Oh don't bring all that up again – it's twenty years ago, and I'm tired hearing about Mam being upset, needing her rest, not to be disturbed, when anything throws you. Anything that happens in this family, I get the blame. It's just not fair.'

He sounded really hard done by and I heard an echo of a child's 'It's not fair, you're picking on me'.

Rosie *[sharply]*: 'I really cannot understand what all the fuss is about. You have to get on in life and make your own way just

like I had to do. And anyway, I don't think it's a bad idea that
Mum and Dad sell the house and take it easy. Dad having been
ill and now retiring, they'd have more money to enjoy life.'

Somehow what Rosie said was much milder than her tone of
voice implied. Whatever the row had been about, or how fierce
a row it had been, she did not want to re-ignite the flames. She
was taking a stance in the middle of the road and saying, in
effect, let's just get on with our lives. In fact, I was finding it
more and more difficult to imagine this group ever having a row
or anything more than a mild disagreement. Then I remembered
that Stephen had been reduced almost to tears on the phone. I
needed to explore further and allow them all space to become
more 'real'.

Trish, the youngest, who was still living with her parents,
had been sitting slightly apart from the others. It occurred to
me that, of the three siblings, she would be the most affected if
any major change occurred. She hadn't spoken yet and the
others had not referred at all to her, not even her parents. She
sat with her head bent, not looking at anyone else. I asked her
what she thought had happened at the birthday party to spark
such a reaction.

Trish *[in a barely audible voice]*: 'I don't really know but I don't
think it had a lot to do with what he actually said. Everyone just
took off and said some very hurtful things.'

Rosie *[interrupting, and I got the sense that she often interrupted]*:
'Oh for heaven's sake. I'm sick and tired of the way you and
Stephen are still so attached to Mum and Dad. It looks as if

you're never going to leave home and make a life for yourself. It's just too cushy for you the way it is.'

Trish [*with tears in her eyes*]: 'You just don't understand! None of you understand. You don't have to live under a microscope, always trying to make things better, and trying to make excuses for everyone. Cushy! You haven't a clue! I should have gone to Australia when I had the chance'.

A stunned silence followed.

Betty: 'Australia? What has Australia got to do with anything?'

I had been aware that Cian, Rosie's son, was becoming more and more uneasy, stretching his sweatshirt sleeves longer and longer, and he suddenly spoke up.

Cian: 'I know what's going on. They're all too tied up in each other's lives. We don't often come to Dublin, but every time we do there are these big family gatherings and they're so boring. We're all meant to be so close and behave as if everything is perfect, pretending that we all love one another all the time and cannot see enough of one another. It's rubbish. Mum cannot stand coming to Dublin, and no one ever comes down to Achill to see us, or asks how we're getting on. There is life outside Dublin you know!'

Stephen: 'Your mother never wanted to go to Achill in the first place!'

Rosie *[looking livid]*: 'How dare you talk about something you don't know the first thing about!'

Betty *[reaching out to Rosie in a placating gesture]*: 'Rosie, we all know you chose to go to Achill to help your friend manage her hostel.'

Alan: 'That's not quite right, dear. Rosie moved out because you and she weren't getting along when she moved back home after the split with Cian's dad.'

There was chaos, with Trish and Betty in tears, Rosie getting more and more angry, Stephen and his father looking bemused, and Cian on the verge of bolting. And only a few minutes before, I had wondered if this family ever had real rows!

Whatever about the group members, I needed some breathing space to reflect on what was happening to this family. From appearing to be a caring family, who maintained initially that they all got on well together, something was unravelling very fast and getting out of control. I suggested it was time to take a break, to have a cup of coffee.

Facilitator's Reflections During the Break

It was obvious that this a family that had skated over emotional exchanges for years, and life-cycle changes and trans-generational fears were never acknowledged. These included Rosie's marriage break-up, Alan's illness and early retirement, Stephen's wish to expand the family business and his parents' fear of the Celtic Tiger, which were somehow absorbed and never dealt with openly.

Now something had surfaced which refused to go away and for which they had no blueprint of how to behave or react. It could be any one of the many topics they had mentioned. The suggestion to sell the family home may have been the trigger, but I did not think it was the underlying cause for the eruption. They appeared to speak to one another without real connection. Were they avoiding uncomfortable truths, fearful of hurting one another with honesty, or had they learned that it was safer to be devious? Whatever the reason, they neither 'meant what they said, nor said what they meant', but this sideways way of speaking was no longer paying dividends. It was instead fomenting rows and fights and, above all, misunderstandings.

Rosie's move to Achill with Cian seemed to be central, not only because it awoke such angry feelings in Rosie right now, but also because it appeared to have created discord between Rosie and her mother at the time. This in turn now led to Alan openly disagreeing with Betty about why Rosie had left home. In addition, Cian's remarks about no one ever visiting them in Achill and his mother hating to go to Dublin further suggested a deeper split within this family than they had hitherto been willing to admit. Trish had mentioned 'some very hurtful things' being said and a complete lack of understanding by the others as to her position. What exactly was her position at home and what was the Australian possibility that appeared to have passed her by? Would she have liked to move out but felt responsible for their parents as the last one living at home? How did she 'get along' with her parents? The hurt and the anger, and even the reverberations from 'the row', appeared to be based mainly among the siblings, with the parents somewhat aloof from the emotional turmoil. The younger generation appeared to be trying to break free from the past, from their parents' fears about money and security, and from the family reluctance to speak plainly and 'say it as it is'.

I was also beginning to wonder about Betty's real relationships within her family – were they as equal and as truly loving as was portrayed, or was she struggling to maintain an outward appearance of harmony? During the break, Alan and Betty sat in the garden, while their children stayed in the meeting room. Was this indicative of anything, something? So many questions, and so little time to try to find some plausible explanations!

The Second Half of the Meeting

When we reconvened, I began by sharing my thoughts:

> **Facilitator**: 'I'd like to let you know what I have heard so far and the impression I have about what is really going on. I am hearing many mixed messages and I am aware that you are finding it increasingly difficult to understand one another's point of view and are hesitant to say how things really are for you, lest you hurt the other person. The result is that you feel they do not understand you. How can they if you aren't willing to tell them honestly? The real state of affairs appears to become visible only when it shoots out in an argument or when you are angry. Would I be right in thinking that the party row was the culmination of many disagreements, and was only different in that it blew everything into the open?'

I left it there. If they were unable to discuss this or recognise it, they would slide away with oblique remarks. However, I hoped they might be able to answer me, the outsider, who wasn't keeping the rules and who was spelling out uncomfortable truths.

To my surprise, Betty was the first to respond.

Betty: 'But you cannot just say things out. It can really do damage. I remember growing up in our village and there was always trouble from people saying things that should never have been mentioned. My uncle's business was ruined because word was spread by a competitor that he 'played around' when he went to Dublin on business. We were always very careful of what we said, both at home and outside. I remember at school no one really knew much about us – I was always afraid of letting out secrets.'

She stopped, hearing the words 'afraid' and 'secrets', and she said somewhat defensively:

'It was safer, and anyway there are always ways around answering difficult questions.'

Alan *[leaping to her defence, although no one was attacking her]*: 'Betty's parents welcomed me into their family with open arms, and into their garage business too, and there was never any comments about where I'd come from. I won't hear a word against them. They were good people and so pleased when we managed to increase business. Of course, they were careful about what was discussed outside the family, and then with the children coming, we had to be careful at home too. It was a small place and tongues wagged.'

I must say I was curious as to what it was they were determined to keep hidden and where Alan 'had come from', but it wasn't really important here. It was the habit of hiding and sidestepping that seemed to require attention, as the children had grown up doing the same thing, although a need to do so may have ceased to exist.

Stephen: 'You were always in the garage, Dad, and I loved working with you, or watching you work. We never said much but I could just say things out. When we went back into the house, Gran and Grandad were always whispering, and I hated that. Do you remember, Mum, the time Gran asked me about school and I told her I hated the history teacher who was picking on me, and the huge row because what would people say if I went on like that. She had always lived in the village, her people were respectable, and I was to mind my p's and q's. Imagine that still in my mind. I was careful after that to tell Gran what she wanted to hear!'

Rosie *[angrily]*: 'Well, Dad was certainly always in the garage, working, doing accounts. He was never in the house, and only Stephen was allowed stay with him. You always made excuses for him, Mam, and you worked so hard. There wasn't much laughter in the house and when he did come in, I used to feel in the way because you both had private jokes and comments, and suddenly it was time for me to go to bed. When Cian was born I really felt I was a burden on you both, and very conscious of the neighbours and what they might be saying. I felt I had to go somewhere, anywhere.'

Cian was looking uncomfortable again. All this history of times before he was born appeared to embarrass him and I wondered had he never heard any of it before.

Suddenly this family was speaking truths openly. Did they feel I had somehow given them permission to talk freely, or was it their mother's discussion of what it was like in a small town – or what? Apparently simple statements were impacting strongly, as if newly discovered.

Betty: 'My dear, I'm sorry if it felt like that. I really was glad to have baby Cian in the house, and you know we'd never have abandoned you when Cian's dad left. But I'd spent so long looking after your Gran and Grandad that I always looked forward to reaching a time when there was just your Dad and myself. No responsibilities, just ourselves to look after. And that must sound awful to you, Trish, but it's different now that you're grown up. You're not a 'responsibility' now, and I do really love having you around.

Trish: 'But I thought you'd be lost without me. I remember Dad saying once he loved the sound of our voices around the house, and now everyone else is gone, I thought it must be very lonely. And you phone me so often at work, Mum, for a chat.'

Betty: 'But when I don't phone you, you ring me. I sometimes worry that you don't have enough of a life outside the family.

And what's this about Australia? Don't tell me you turned something down just to look after us, because there's no need at all.'

Trish: 'But I've always preferred being at home with you in the evening rather than going to noisy discos and pubs. When Ann and Amanda went off to Sydney, I couldn't bear the thought of making new friends.'

Betty *[incredulously]*: 'But that was six or seven years ago!'

Trish: 'It's so hard making friends.'

She sounded quite flat and somehow adrift. Her tears were gone, and she was looking at her parents as if she'd never seen them before. From saying so vehemently that no one understood her and her position, she now found that she herself didn't understand what was going on either. Stephen, who had started all this, was also looking bemused. Where was the row and the fighting, and his clumsy remarks which had ignited all this? Through sharing their history and their feelings on a new level, these family members were beginning to recognise each other with a new honesty.

Cian: 'You sound like me, Trish. I always feel I have to look after Mum in Achill, and that I could never leave home because she needs me. And then I think I'm crazy because everyone has to leave home at some time. So maybe we can talk about it, Mum, because there's a course I'd really like to do, but it's in Dublin, not in Galway.'

The Brown Family: Family legacies

We had used up all our time, and I thought that a summary would be helpful for this family, leaving as they were with so much new insight. In a way nothing had been 'sorted', but hopefully they had found the beginning of a different way of communicating and sharing ideas.

> **Facilitator**: 'We have come to the end of our session and perhaps I could outline what I have heard. You appear to have inherited, unknowingly, a rule that insisted that straight talking could be hurtful to others, so you lived by assuming that you knew what others were thinking and feeling. Dealing with problems indirectly ensured that the family remained in touch and supportive, even if there were differences that were never discussed. The needs of each of you as individuals were never recognised or spoken about, and eventually obligations which each of you assumed were real and necessary became punitive and led to misunderstandings over the years. Perhaps you can each take some time to consider our discussions today, and try then to find a way of sharing what you have discovered with the others.'

> **Rosie** *[immediately and with some relief]*: 'Let's all meet up again when I'm in Dublin in a couple of weeks for Christmas, and sure we'll be in touch on and off until then.'

Conclusion

And that was that. They slowly and amicably dispersed, saying thank you over and over, as if I'd done something wonderful! And maybe I had, although I was not aware of having done much. Somehow our meeting had been a catalyst, at just the right time for this family. They appeared to have been on the brink of disintegration, while all the time wishing one another well, and therefore had been willing to avail of this brief opportunity to share and uncover some home truths, hitherto invisible to them, although perhaps obvious to an outsider. I was left to marvel yet again at the strange and wonderful ways and remedies which families can create to reach new beginnings and new ways of communicating.

Note

1. Ledwidge, Francis, 'In the Mediterranean: Going to the War' in *The Complete Poems*, NY: Brentano's, 1919, p. 175.

– 7 –

The Murphy Family:
Secret histories

To know that, like a bird down on a branch
stray, unbeckoned, out of a wide sky
has come to them the moment of accord.[1]

Introduction

For a facilitator, remaining detached from and uninvolved in
the family problems can be difficult in many cases, but one of
the most challenging is to stay non-judgemental when a family
presents whose way of living and values/beliefs are far removed
from your own. It is hard to remain tolerant when a person is
inveighing against single mothers, people with different skin
colour or religion, and generally displaying deep-set prejudices.
But I have invited these family members to be open and
honest, and will I now judge them for that very honesty
because it doesn't sit easily with my own value system, judge
them because they are judging others? Families can become
very set in their ways and can live for years, unknowingly, in
the shadow of past history. The prejudices and fears which
result from previous experiences, many years in the past, can be
thrown into prominence through a series of current events and

can strongly influence the manner in which family members communicate. This past history can even dictate family values, which can be challenged by younger members who have no knowledge of the reasons behind the household rules. They revolt against what they see as merely old-fashioned laws designed to thwart their dreams. In any examination of why or how these laws have come about, the children can begin to understand their parents better, and the parents in turn can examine their own choices more thoroughly and decide if they wish to change. Perhaps the most important element offered in this kind of work is safety – safety from ridicule, attack, criticism, judgement – and within this safe space, participants risk saying what would perhaps be unthinkable elsewhere.

Initial Contact

Ray Murphy contacted me about difficulties his family were having in coming to terms with a long-term relationship between his eldest daughter, Emma, and Max from Eastern Europe. Sounding quiet-spoken but deeply worried, he explained how distressed Emma was at what she perceived as a total lack of understanding he and her mother, Ann, had for her partner. He had a second daughter, Fiona, who was becoming more and more withdrawn as a result of the ongoing conflict in the house.

Max had recently proposed marriage to Emma and had come to stay on the family farm for the summer. After only two weeks a crisis had arisen, and Max had left their house suddenly and taken a flight back to his own country. Ray told me Emma was very distressed, losing a lot of weight (which she could ill afford to do) and was talking about going to live with Max abroad. Ann was distraught and angry, and was threatening to ban them both from her house.

Ray needed help. The Murphys had inadvertently been caught up in events that severely challenged their hidden prejudices and fears. Having lived comparatively secluded lives up to now, modern Ireland was presenting them with a changed landscape, filled with foreign faces and languages, and many different nationalities. Their towns, shops and streets no longer offered the familiar, but demanded adjustment to the new and the different.

However, I sensed from the outset that their present difficulties contained more than mere adjustment to the new surroundings, but posed some more fundamental threat to the family's – or more accurately, to the mother's – values and beliefs on which her life and living were based. The threat *as perceived* was so much greater than appeared to the outside eye, which saw difference and change, but nothing particularly life threatening. I felt there was a lot I was not hearing, or not understanding.

The First Half of the Meeting

When we all met they nervously sat where I indicated. Ray was tall and thin and weather-beaten; Ann was comfortable looking and wearing a smart outfit; Emma was indeed very thin and looked most unhappy; while Fiona presented as reluctant, bored and apprehensive, all at the same time. I introduced myself, spoke briefly about confidentiality and how our time together would be structured, and then invited Ray (as instigator of the meeting) to outline the trouble as he saw it.

Ray: 'During the last twelve months we've all become more and more unhappy, and this has become really bad since Max came to stay for the summer.'

As Emma began to protest, he raised his hand and said:

'I'm not blaming Max, but his arrival seems to have been a turning point – and it's been downhill all the way. Since you met him in college last year you've been inseparable, but we only really saw that when he came to stay. I'm sure he's a fine young man *[he said this with some lack of conviction]*, but you've changed so much. He seems to demand all your time and you're never free to help in the house or on the farm, as you always used. Your mother is finding it all very hard.'

He paused and I felt this had been a long speech for Ray. Their close, unchanging family circle had been breached and change had come without his invitation. He spoke quietly without raising his voice, but with authority, and I wondered what he really thought about Max, the foreigner, perhaps even the intruder.

Ann had no such quietness. She was angry and didn't care who knew it, and she spoke directly to me:

Ann: 'They got engaged at Easter without asking us. When Max came to stay for three months I understood he would help us with the workload. That's the only reason I agreed to put him up – an extra pair of hands when we were so busy. But no! I asked him and asked him to do the washing-up, the cooking, bringing in the cattle, helping with the visitors, but it never really happened. He always had an excuse. He spent his days at the computer and Emma with him, as often as not.

'He was lazy and uncooperative, and he has turned Emma from being a girl who gets on with everyone to someone who never goes out, but sits whispering to Max all day long. I don't know how they behave in his country, but it's obviously not our way.'

Ann was prepared to go on and on. Max and Emma hadn't asked permission to become engaged and his country had different standards to those in her Ireland. The old ways were certainly being challenged.

Ann: 'He doesn't know how to behave in a normal home. Look at how he demanded to be driven to the train station when he stormed off. You have so many friends in Ireland, I cannot see why you chose someone from so far away. Your father and I were neighbours; everyone knew us and we knew everyone, and we never went very far afield.'

Ann showed great inner control and I wondered if this was disguising some unacknowledged fear. She seemed ready to go on but Ray said: 'Hold on a moment, Ann', and Emma now had space to talk.

Emma [white-faced and distressed]: 'You're so unfair. You're asking me to make a choice between Max and my family. You just don't give him a chance. [Directly to facilitator] I really do love my family and I've been so happy all my life, but now I love Max too. When we were in college it was fine, because I just wouldn't listen to any criticism of him, and anyway they hadn't met him. I thought once they knew him, it would be different, but the few weeks he was here, it was terrible. Dad's right: whenever Max and Mam had words, it was awful. *[To Ann]* He really felt you despised him and that there was nothing he could do about it. It wasn't his fault he wasn't Irish. They were quite poor and he grew up in a city flat, and he was terrified of the animals. He was so afraid that he'd do something wrong, that he ended up doing nothing at all.

'And I don't know what you said to him that last night, because he wouldn't tell me, but he was really hurt, and he may never come back now.' *[She began to cry]*

Ann *[somewhat defensively]*: 'I don't know why you think it's all my fault – I just told him that we were different here and that he would always find it difficult to fit in, and that would make life difficult for you. And that's true. I told him you'd be better off with someone of your own kind, and that there were lots of young men around willing to take his place!'

In that moment I found myself almost disliking Ann. However fearful she was of losing her daughter, I found it hard to comprehend how she could have been so cruel to Max, and how she could now continue that cruelty towards Emma. At the same time, I could not take the risk of my prejudice blocking my ability to hear what was really disturbing Ann, who was also a member of this family. By becoming aware of and acknowledging my feelings (not without a struggle), I was able to put them aside and regain my neutrality and tolerance in order to continue in my role as facilitator.

Emma [*speaking directly to her father*]: 'I'm tired trying to protect Max from you all and the way you're constantly criticising him. He's gentle and he's kind and I love him!'

The words came like a challenge, a gauntlet thrown down in defence of Max. I got a sense of what it must be like in the Murphy household lately, as Emma and Ann threw words and accusations at each other like stones. I guessed their relationship had never been easy, but now that Max had come on the scene, the usual friction had flared into outright battle.

And now, to our surprise, Fiona spoke up:

Fiona: 'I don't know why I'm here. I only know I seem to have lost Emma and everything lands on me now. Surely if Emma really loves Max, that's all that really matters. I thought love was meant to make you happy, and now the whole house is miserable with Mam angry and Emma crying all the time. Dad gets on with it because he has to. Just let's all stop fighting. Max cannot help where he's from and Emma cannot help loving him.'

I wished we could all have the clarity of vision and the conviction of the young, that love equalled happiness and that was all there was to it!

Ann: 'I just want things to be back to where they were, and I certainly don't want any of us leaving the country. There was more than enough of that when I was growing up – look at all my sisters in America. We almost never see them. Bad enough all the foreigners here now without having to go away ourselves.'

There was something more here that I could not put my finger on, so I took a risk and spoke directly to Ann:

Facilitator: 'I can see you're very angry with the whole scene, but somehow I get the impression that you're frightened too – and I don't understand that.'

For some minutes Ann struggled to respond and I felt she might deny my suggestion outright. When she spoke, it was quietly but still angrily.

Ann: 'I was in my Granny's house the day they heard my aunt had run off with a foreign student and gone to live abroad. She never came back. Not a day went by but my Granny spoke about her, how she'd been stolen away, snatched from her family and country. My Granny was quite dramatic and I stayed with her a lot when I was small, and I remember her wailing. I don't remember my aunt, but I had a picture of her in my head, and I could never make up my mind whether she was a victim or a "hussy", as my Granny called her. I do know she caused great unhappiness and I used to hate her because I loved my Granny. I've been thinking of her a lot lately, and I wish I'd met her when I grew up. They never kept a picture of her or spoke about her later, and it was as if she'd died – and perhaps she did. I just don't know.'

And now she was more sad than angry, and her family stared at her in amazement.

> **Fiona**: 'What was her name? Why did you never tell us about her?'

Ann made no reply. She appeared to be momentarily withdrawn into herself. It appeared to me that the mood of the group had shifted from struggle to consideration of what had been disclosed, so I suggested that we have a cup of tea, and everyone looked relieved. Because of the intensity of concentration, these meetings are physically draining as well as mentally tiring, and the break is a time to relax and stretch tired muscles.

Facilitator's Reflections During the Break

I had much to reflect on during the break. I realised that Ann's anger masked this hitherto unacknowledged fear that she could lose Emma forever, totally, as had happened with her aunt. This was a secret from her family of origin, so deeply embedded that she had never thought to tell her own children. It was a secret that had vanished from sight, but had not gone away. She saw foreigners as disrupting the status quo, and the scourge of mass emigration as she was growing up had added its mark. Change of any kind was a threat; it was best always to stay close to home and not risk adventures of any kind. Going away or abroad was always 'bad' and nothing could change that.

Ann had managed very well with the familiar and the unchanging, but her basic beliefs in the merit of hard work and families sticking together whatever happened were being undermined by these latest events in her family. It was unclear how her relationship with her family would survive what appeared to be on the horizon. While it was good for her to be able to articulate her rage, it was important too that she step away from it and see that it originated in her fears. It was always going to be hard for her to let Emma go when she sought independence, but with the arrival of Max, all her fears came together to threaten her.

I had a strong sense that this family was deeply embedded in the conventions of a rural family of the twentieth century. They had moved ahead by creating a pet farm to supplement the farm income and the two daughters helped out. With no son to inherit or to help with the farm as they got older, it would be logical for them to hope that either Emma or Fiona might marry a man who would be interested in the farm. Max was neither suitable nor interested, coming as he did from a city background, and knowing nothing of a rural way of life in Ireland or elsewhere. He in no way fulfilled any expectation they might have of him becoming involved in the family enterprise. However, since this had not been alluded to, it was not appropriate to introduce it. I would keep it in mind and be aware that it might colour further discussions.

Emma was at the centre of the discord, and she was not comfortable with her position. She appeared to be more unhappy than angry, and quite unable to understand her mother's or her father's opposition. Her view was centred on Max. If they disagreed with anything at all, with anything she said or did, then they were against Max. Understandably she saw no wider picture, her focus was on the here and now. Max had left, had been driven away by her parents, and if they didn't change, she too was gone. She believed the choice was stark unless her mother changed completely. She would lose either her family or her fiancé, but there really wasn't a choice – Max was her future, with or without her family.

Fiona appeared to be deeply embedded in her family, but was particularly connected to Emma. It seemed possible that if Emma left home in anger, then Fiona would shortly follow, whereas if Emma could maintain a good connection, then Fiona might find it easier to do so too. Being young, she was quite willing to be distracted from family turmoil by images of true love and stories of missing relatives.

Ray, although quiet, appeared to exercise power without effort. It was he who had requested and arranged our meeting, and the others were all here at his request. I doubted if any one of them had come willingly. I was interested to note that although both Ray and Ann had a deeply shared concern for Max and Emma's relationship, it was Ray who had taken the initiative to convene the meeting. What transpired within the family in this meeting with me might, in the long run, be a more effective and longer-lasting lever to change Ann's attitude. I got the sense that Ray was able to see a larger future picture than Ann. He would like to see the girls happy and appeared to be more willing to temper his own feelings about the idea of their leaving home by considering a situation where they had left but remained strongly attached and visited often.

I was intrigued to think that, while understanding Ann's fears, he may have needed acknowledgement of these to come from an outsider, or from the family unit as a whole, rather than just from himself. If he were to take charge and issue ultimatums about living in harmony, a truce might result but it would probably be an uneasy compromise. Any effort made by Ann and Emma as a result of an 'expert's' input might have a better chance of success.

Yet while all of this might indeed be true, it was very much guesswork on my part. I often hold tentative ideas in the back of my mind, although never viewing them as facts. These can offer a creative source from which I can help the family to better understand themselves and their situation. However, as they will not always be accurate, it is wise to offer only glimpses of them. It is then possible to gauge the reaction (be it incomprehension or recognition) of the family members to these ideas and either withdraw them from circulation or proceed with further exploration.

The Second Half of the Meeting

As is usual at this point, when we all sat down together again, the atmosphere was quite different. It seemed calmer, as if some kind of truce had been called. I outlined what I had heard from each of them.

Facilitator: 'You all seem so unhappy as a family, yet the reasons for this are different for each of you. Ray, you appear to be most upset at the fighting within the family, and the general misery. You are also willing to meet each of the others half-way. Ann, I hear your fear around the possibility of Emma emigrating and your fear also of outsiders threatening the family, as it appeared to be with your aunt, and the anger this generates within you.

'Emma, I hear you saying that no matter what happens, you will be the loser, and that is a dreadful position to be in. If you stay at home you lose Max; if you stay with Max you lose your family. Fiona, you dread that you will lose Emma and the family will never be the same again.

'Such a lot of fear, and especially fear of loss. Having acknowledged this, can we look at whether the future can temper that loss or is there any way to include some gain as well?'

This was a longer speech than I usually make, but it seemed both necessary and appropriate here. Emma replied immediately:

Emma: 'I'd like Mam and Dad to accept Max. They don't have to love him and, while he is different, deep down he's a good person and we'd like to marry in a few years. I might visit his folks to get to know them, but I'd like to live in Ireland too, Mam. I don't plan on going anywhere, except for a holiday. I spoke to Max on the phone last night. Perhaps it would help if I agreed to stay at home and help for the next six weeks, and then I hope to join Max at his home for a month. I'll come back to go to college at the end of September.'

Having heard what her family had to say in our discussion, Emma appeared to have recovered somewhat, and was now making a plan which she offered to them. Her choice was no longer the stark one of 'either family or Max', but rather one of how to pick her way between the two.

Ann: 'And will you agree that Max stays at home and does not join you in college next year?'

Emma: 'That's daft, Mam, and you know it. Just don't push it.'

There was a note in her voice that gave a warning that to ask for more from her would mean losing all. No magic solution had been found, but they understood one another better. The tensions and worries, the angers and jealousies, were no longer simmering below the surface, but had been acknowledged and declared, and they were freer to make decisions, seeming to understand that shift and compromise were needed now. Ann still found it difficult to even mention change and she looked as if she was about to rekindle the row, but Ray intervened.

Ray: 'That sounds good to me – gives us all a breathing space to think things over. I'd like Emma to be less torn apart. I realise you love Max, but you love us too. *[Directly to Ann]* Times are changing and it's no longer the place we grew up in. Surely we can all mark time until she's finished in college in a couple of years. We have been afraid of things changing and putting off thinking about it, but it would be dreadful if we now lost all because we were afraid of losing some – if you know what I mean.'

Ann: 'But why do things have to change? Aren't we all right as we are? I feel something dreadful is going to happen and there's nothing I can do.'

After a silence I asked:

Facilitator: 'Do you always feel future change is bad? Is there no possibility at all of something good ever happening?'

Ann: 'None. None at all. How could there be?'

And here was the centre of her fear: helplessness in the face of oncoming disaster and not being able to do anything about it. Even Fiona felt a need to challenge this.

Fiona: 'Come on, Mam. Of course good things can happen. Remember before we started the pet farm and all was gloom and doom, but everything worked out so well. And Dad getting the grant to build the milking parlour. You always expect the worst.'

Ray, as if he were heading off further angry exchanges, said somewhat abruptly:

Ray: 'Well, you've given us a lot to think about and to talk about. Maybe things will be clearer now.'

And he stood up to go, ending our meeting quite decisively.

Conclusion

I got a sense that something had been accomplished, some goal achieved, although to me it was all still up in the air. So we all stood and the family began to file out, Emma looking stronger,

Ann still disgruntled and Fiona making her escape, as they murmured their thanks and goodbyes. Ray looked the most satisfied of them all as we shook hands. Even more than usual, I was left asking questions that would never be answered.

Note

1. Colum, Padraic, 'Images of Departure' in *Images of Departure*, Ireland: The Dolmen Press, 1969, p. 10.

– 8 –

Conclusion

We must learn to live together as brothers or perish together as fools.[1]

Families in the Community

In the past, families consulted a wise person when decisions needed to be taken – an older aunt, a grandparent or godmother – to provide wisdom or solutions. In literature and in folklore, the role of this wise person was acknowledged and appreciated, and they were consulted in troubled times.

Our communities have lost much of their connectedness, due to changing social, geographical and economic reasons, and those in dispute, particularly within a family, no longer seek out a wise person. Indeed, families often do not even perceive their need for help, but struggle on towards collapse – of themselves, their health and the very fabric of the family to which they belong. This work tries to help these fragmented and less permanent families in their search for solutions.

Meeting Individual Needs

Having read this book, you, the reader, may wonder how you can apply this to your own family situation. Perhaps you could ask yourself some of the following questions.

- What is the problem?
- How serious is it? (score in scale of 1–10)
- Does it need to be dealt with immediately, some time soon, later?
- What might happen if action is not taken?
- Would that make the situation worse?
- Is it the kind of problem that some of the family could resolve or does it need everyone's attention?
- Could the problem be resolved at the next family gathering?
- Would a meeting with a facilitator for a few hours be enough?
- Would the problem benefit from the intervention of an outside agency, e.g. social services?
- Do you think a facilitator might help you become clearer about identifying the problem and what, if any, course of action to take?
- Might you see the meeting with a facilitator as part of the process or an end in itself?

The way you answer any of the above may help clarify what course of action, if any, you might consider taking.

During these meetings, the facilitator may hear echoes of the childhood needs of the family members. An individual who failed to find their voice or someone to listen to them as a child in the hurly-burly of daily family interaction may be still lost and silenced as an adult. Receiving opportunity and encouragement to speak may release a family member from years of non-involvement with the others. A phrase used by Helen Bamber, who worked with victims of torture after World War II, illustrates the active nature of good listening: '... you could listen people into telling their stories ...'[2]

The need to be understood is as strong as the need to be loved. We try so hard to explain ourselves, our thoughts and our actions. We expend effort and words trying to ensure that others understand 'exactly' what we mean, down to the tiniest nuance and fleck of feeling. No half-measures, no smudging, and we often cease to truly listen, because we are so caught up with explaining ourselves. In these family meetings, each person gets a chance to explain themselves and how they view the 'problem'. They are then required to listen to the others, each in turn, explaining how it looks from their stance.

Meeting the Family's Needs

While every family is unique and has its own familial signature, many of these meetings follow a similar pattern: meeting, angry exchanges, denial, letting off steam, moving to hearing others' points of view, calming down to discuss options, plans and decisions towards progress. Our task is to help clear the obstacles to whatever goals they have in view.

Of course there are exceptions. On one occasion, a family consisting of one parent and four siblings used their time to hurt and wound each other. They barely allowed the facilitator room to speak and carried on as if they were not there. They shouted and said cruel things, until one of the siblings walked out (the one who had arranged the meeting). The remaining four participants then set in to criticise one another and the girl who had left, until after about an hour they all stormed out. The facilitator sat in the room for a long time trying to recover, and wondering why they had come! These people liked neither themselves nor anyone else, and bore goodwill to no-one.

Sometimes we hear the statement 'I'm only here because …', denoting an unwillingness to take responsibility either for discussion or for any decision. This is well illustrated by Derek in the O'Reilly family saying, 'I don't know why I'm here. I didn't want to come and I'm sorry already that I did … Where's the point?' This kind of statement often stems from a learned defensiveness – protective barriers against involvement. There is also the defensiveness against any criticism of ourselves or our parents. Some people maintain that they had 'a perfect childhood', despite proceeding to speak of unkindness and cruelty. To continue to believe in this perfection may be safer and less threatening than permitting any criticism of the loved, and powerful, parents. In a way, the belief in a perfect childhood may bury the real feelings that might be too painful to unearth.

Our Meetings

These meetings are not unique, but they resemble those meetings that many families instigate in order to manage decisions in a democratic way. Difficulties are discussed in common, and outcomes are agreed or changed by agreement of the group. Similarly we have found that working in this way can be successful with small groups such as voluntary bodies, parish associations, clubs and so on. The idea of such discussion and facilitation is not new, but we believe that its brevity (three hours) and its central belief in the right and ability of the group to create and plan its own solutions are different. The application of the ideas of basic respect for each person, the focus on clarity and understanding, the listening to what is not being said as well as to what is said – all this comes together in a format that is easier for today's families to grasp and to utilise. (It is interesting that some similarities exist between this work and the idea of 'collaborative practice', recently introduced by the Legal Aid Board to try to resolve family law matters by communication and negotiation, rather than having recourse to the law courts.)

The Facilitator

The facilitator needs to truly *believe* in the effectiveness of this once-off session or they will convince neither themselves nor the group with which they are working. As relationship is of primary importance, it is essential that they, as facilitators, are positive and enthusiastic. Since the work is also filled with uncertainty, they need to hold confident certainty and also be prepared at all times for surprises – to expect the unexpected.

They need to *trust* in themselves and in the probability of a satisfactory outcome; they need to have faith in their ability to support these family members, and in the ability of the group to reach a solution to their difficulties.

Identification and exploration will usually culminate in some resolution for the family. Solutions are rarely either neat or comprehensive, but the combined wisdom and willing discussion of the group can almost always identify a desirable next step. New and creative suggestions appear, which quite often win the approval or acceptance of even the most resistant and argumentative of family members!

By facilitating the exploration and expression of 'real' emotions and feelings beneath the protective facades, the expectation is that each group member will allow themselves to truly see how life (and this problem in particular) appears to the others. If you can, in this way, freely and openly discuss and acknowledge the differences in values and beliefs held in your family, then dialogue and discussion will follow. From this new understanding and perception of the problem, new ways of dissolving the discord can literally transform your family relationships.

Notes

1   King, Martin Luther at St Louis, USA, 22 March 1964 in *Oxford Book of Quotations*, Oxford University Press, 1999.
2   Belton, Neil, *The Good Listener,* UK: Phoenix, 1998/199, p. 109.

Bibliography

Asen, Eia, *Family Therapy for Everyone*, UK: BBC Books, 1995.

Belton, Neil, *The Good Listener*, UK: Phoenix, 1998/1999.

Dallos, Rudi, *Family Belief Systems, Therapy and Change*, UK: Open University Press, 1991.

Jones, Elsa, *Family Systems Therapy: Developments in the Milan-Systemic Therapies*, UK: John Wiley & Sons, 1993.

Knowles, Elizabeth (ed.), *The Oxford Dictionary of Quotations*, UK: Oxford University Press, 1999.

Levitt, Brian E. (ed.), *Embracing Non-Directivity*, UK: PCCS Books, 2005.

McGraw, Phil, *Family First*, UK: Simon and Schuster, 2005.

O'Farrell, Ursula, *Considering Counselling*, Ireland: Veritas, 2004.

O'Farrell, Ursula, *Courage to Change*, Ireland: Veritas, 1999.

O'Farrell, Ursula, *First Steps in Counselling*, Ireland: Veritas, 1988/2006.

Rivett, Mark and Street, Eddy, *Family Therapy in Focus*, UK: Sage, 2003.

Rogers, Carl R., *A Way of Being*, NY: Houghton Mifflin Co., 1980.

Rogers, Carl R., *On Becoming a Person,* UK: Constable, 1961/1988.

Satir, Virginia, *Peoplemaking,* USA: Science and Behavior Books Inc., 1972/1998.

Sharry, John, *Counselling Children, Adolescents and Families,* UK: Sage, 2004.

Skynner, Robin and Cleese, John, *Families and How to Survive Them,* UK: Vermilion/Ebury Press, 1983/1997.

Tulku Rinpoche, Akong, *Taming the Tiger,* UK: Rider, 1987/1994.

Walrond-Skinner, Sue, *Family Therapy: The Treatment of Natural Systems,* UK: Routledge and Kegan Paul, 1977

Meeting Space

Meeting Space is a service established by Sarah McLoughlin and Ursula O'Farrell to assist families such as those presented in this book. If you would like further information, please contact Meeting Space at: sjkka@eircom.net or uofarrell@eircom.net.